Anonymous

The Garden

Or, familiar instructions for the laying out and management of a flower garden

Anonymous

The Garden
Or, familiar instructions for the laying out and management of a flower garden

ISBN/EAN: 9783337069087

Printed in Europe, USA, Canada, Australia, Japan

Cover: Foto ©Lupo / pixelio.de

More available books at **www.hansebooks.com**

ARGEMONE GRANDIFLORA. *Large-flowered Mexican Poppy.*

THE GARDEN;

OR

FAMILIAR INSTRUCTIONS

FOR THE

LAYING OUT AND MANAGEMENT OF A FLOWER GARDEN.

WITH

ILLUSTRATIVE ENGRAVINGS ON WOOD.

PHILADELPHIA:
J. B. LIPPINCOTT & CO.
1861.

Entered according to Act of Congress, in the year 1854,

BY S. G. GOODRICH,

in the Clerk's Office of the District Court of Massachusetts.

PREFACE.

There is no pursuit which combines in a higher degree utility and pleasure than that of gardening. It is therefore desirable that young persons should very early form a taste for it. If in childhood they have their attention turned to it, and learn the names of flowers and plants, and the modes of cultivating them, they will not only be likely to relish the pursuit in after life, but they will gain a kind of knowledge, which they will find gratifying as well as profitable.

This work is designed for youth, and it is hoped it may be the means of drawing some of them into a taste for the innocent and cheerful and useful pursuit of gardening. It is hoped also that these pages may serve to communicate some valuable and pleasing knowledge to older readers.

CONTENTS.

LETTER I.

JANUARY.

Directions for laying out a Flower Garden.—Dutch gardens.—Turf border.—South wall, and South border Climbers.—Arbour.—Designs for Centre Bed.—Borders, nature of Soil requisite, Draining, Compost.—American border.—Distance at which American shrubs should be planted; why planted in bog earth.—Different plants used for edging borders.—Instructions for Edging.—Gravel Walks.—Distinction between Shrubs, Annuals, &c. . . . . Page 15.

LETTER II.

FEBRUARY.

Edging to borders.—Hints for planting Herbaceous Plants, as to height, colour and time of flowering.—

CONTENTS.

Distance to be observed between roots and patches of seed. Tools most necessary for a young gardener.—Evergreens, and their treatment.—Roots of Flowering Shrubs.—Pruning.—Turf.—Instructions for sowing Auricula and Polyanthus seeds, and Hardy Annuals.—Marking Sticks . . . . . Page 35.

LETTER III.

MARCH.

Succession bed.—Bed of Scarlet Anemonies and Purple Orchises.—Advice as to Florists' flowers.—How to make border for Ranunculuses.—Garden made gay by Annuals.—Method of raising Half-hardy Annuals.—Those to be sown at the end of the month.—Seed bed for Perennials and Biennials.—Size of plants.—American shrubs and evergreens to be transplanted.—Rose-trees . . . . Page 47.

LETTER IV.

APRIL.

Dreariness of the garden at this season.—Flowers in bloom —Change produced in habits of plants by climate.

—Dividing herbaceous plants.—Annuals to be sown in April.—Plant out, or pot, Half-hardy Annuals.—Method.—Flowers in bloom during the month.—Edging of Hearts-ease.—Rockwork.—Tie up and protect Hyacinths and Tulips.—Cheap awning for them.—Reasons why plants require light.—Tender Annuals to be sown.—Raise Balm of Gilead and Verbena.—Directions for growing the common sorts of Carnations   Page 58.

LETTER V.

MAY.

Basket sent.—Contents.—Roots of Dahlias, &c. preserved during winter, to be planted and propagated.—New Annuals.—Green-house plants to be put in warm border.—Cuttings to be made of plants sent.—Cheiranthus Tristis and other plants scentless during the day.—Directions for making and striking cuttings of different plants.—Flowers in bloom during the month.—Plant Indian Pinks, Stocks, and tender Annuals.—Shade and water them.—Sow Half-hardy Annuals.—Work to be done during the month   .   .   .   .   Page 75.

CONTENTS.

LETTER VI.

JUNE.

Neatness of the Dutch.—Hand weeding.—Hoeing.—Raking.—Tying up herbaceous plants.—Sticking them.—Take up Bulbs to dry.—Reason why they should be taken up; leaves not to be injured.—Directions for striking Pink pipings, cuttings of China, Moss, and other Roses.—Carnation cuttings, and slips of different plants, how to make.—Keep Garden neat.—Plant Perennials and Biennials in beds.—Plant bulbs of Bella Donna, Guernsey Lily, and Colchicum, &c.—Make cuttings of Greenhouse plants.—Propagate Chrysanthemums.—Instructions for making Flower Baskets, Ornamental Vases and Tables.—Clip Edgings and Weed Gravel.—Tie up Carnations and Pink plants and their pods.—Flowers in bloom —Sow Brompton Stock Seed, for the next year
Page 92.

LETTER VII.

JULY.

Fruits of industry.—Gardening considered as a rational amusement.—On order.—Flowers in bloom during the month.—How to make layers of Carnations.—Reason why so made.—May be raised by Pipings.—Varieties of Carnations.—Work to be done in Garden.—Gather Seeds, and dry them.—How to make a descriptive Catalogue of Carnations.—To raise cuttings of Green-house plants and others.—Seedling Pinks.—On Watering.—Take up Bulbous Roots.—Tree Roses.—Method of budding Rose Stocks . . . . . Page 115

LETTER VIII.

AUGUST.

The Tree Carnation.—Strike cuttings of it.—Poor persons fond of flowers.—Artisans great Florists.—Distinction between Gardeners, Florists, and Botanists; often confounded.—Botany; its advantages.--Continue to lay Carnations.—Treatment of those potted.—Lay Indian Pinks.—Reason why weak plants require shading, and air is excluded from cuttings.—Raise bulbous roots from seed.—Ferraria tigridia.—Divide Herbaceous plants.—Transplant Seedling Biennials, &c.—Shade newly planted Seedlings.—Sow Mignonette in pots.—Divide Rock plants.—Plants in flower.—Lobelias; easily propagated
Page 132

LETTER IX.

SEPTEMBER.

Carnations.—Transplant Pink Pipings, if rooted.—Directions for making Box edgings.—Collecting Seeds.—Plant out and pot Brompton Stocks.—American Border.—Prepare Turf for use.—Plants in flower.—Russian Violets.—Carnations; how prevented from bursting.—An old tree made ornamental.—Use of Latin names in Botany . . . . Page 153.

LETTER X.

OCTOBER.

In-door amusements more fitted to the winter season than gardening.—Prepare Bulb bed; how to plant it.—Narcissus planted under a wall.—Treatment of Bulbs which are to blow in pots.—Reasons for such treatment.—Bulbous plants natives of dry climates.—Sand put to drain the roots.—Planting Tulips and Anemonies.—Take up Green-house plants.—Object of Cold Frames.—Clearing borders, and dividing herbaceous roots.—Prune flower shrubs, and put sticks to them.—Care to be observed in pruning shrubs to be transplanted.—Plants in bloom during the month . . . . Page 163.

CONTENTS.

LETTER XI.

NOVEMBER.

Dig up borders, and trim roots.—Prune shrubs; clean sticks.—Take off suckers.—Dig in dead leaves or rotten dung.—Plant Tulips and Ranunculuses; protect them from frost and heavy rains.—Collect leaves.—Sweep and roll gravel walks.—Attend to Carnation beds, and Alpine plants.—Bodies which retain heat longest.—Effect of cold without snow, on Alpine plants.—Snow preserves plants in Alpine regions.—Alpine and American Springs compared.—Cold frame a substitute for snow.—Plant Alpine plants in dry situations.—Take up Dahlia roots, &c.—Plants in bloom . . . . . Page 178.

LETTER XII.

DECEMBER.

Vegetable physiology attempted to be defined; its importance as a science.—Gardening leads to love of order and neatness.—Distinguished men have been fond of gardening.—Sweep and roll during the whole winter.—Attend to the frames, and prevent the plants in them from growing too freely.—Conclusion . . Page 192

THE GARDEN.

LETTER I.

January.

Your request that I should send you a monthly journal of my garden, and give instructions for the laying out and management of your own, gave me great pleasure. I shall indeed be happy to give you all the information I possess. My garden still continues a favourite amusement and occupation. As the season is not yet sufficiently advanced to make a mere journal interesting, I intend to devote this and the two following letters to the instructions necessary for the formation of the garden, and to give you the result of all my experience on the subject. From my recollections of the shrubberies of ———, and from your description, I know exactly where the plot of ground allotted to you is situated. It is an oblong square piece, surrounded on two sides by the kitchen garden wall and the paling of the orchard, and, on the other two, by the nursery, which is irregular on the longest side opposite the wall. It is a delightful spot, and so well sheltered, that the tenderest of our out-door plants will live and thrive there. I rejoice that it is quite shut out from the rest of the garden, as this will enable you to give it a character as a whole, without its being interfered with by the arrangements of your neighbours. I think, that as three sides of it are perfectly straight, the fourth should be made straight also, and then laid out in formal beds, in the Dutch style, which is an excellent plan where there is but little space, and flowers only are intended to be cultivated; for though this method of laying out a garden supposes the intention of making each bed contain only one kind of flowers, yet I consider that it may be equally adapted to a mixed flower garden.

Notwithstanding what I have stated, I am well aware of the beauty of the wild and irregular in the arrangement of pleasure grounds; but this, to produce a good effect, requires space; and, to be really beautiful, there should be inequality of surface, and the power of producing a variety of form without confusion. It is indispensable, also, that the whole plan should not be seen at once, but this, with your little nook, you cannot hope to accomplish; I recommend you, therefore, to content yourself with neatness and regularity; conceiving your main object is to have as much room to show off the flowers as possible.

Now for the rules as to the making the garden—the irregular piece, which you take off to make the parallelogram, or oblong square, may be planted with our own American shrubs; these, you will observe, grow well in the shade, and will not be injured by being close to the plantations. As soon as you have given the ground a regular form, make a border three feet wide in front of the wall, which I propose you should cover with creepers, and such beautiful flowering shrubs as, in this climate, require to be grown against a wall for protection; and I think, as show is your object, you will not mind sacrificing the two old peach trees, which cover it at present. This wall being towards the south, renders it invaluable. However bare and ugly it may appear at present, you will be content when it is covered with the flowers of the *Bignonia radicans,* or trumpet flower, the jasmine, Zinnia, a beautiful flower, the *Calycanthus precox,* or scented allspice, (which blows in the middle of the winter, and is so fragrant, that a single blossom is sufficient to perfume a whole room,) the mule and common passion flowers; and many others that I can name to you.

After planting the shrubs, which are to grow against the wall, the remainder of the border must be devoted to such delicate plants as require a warm situation, particularly to tender bulbs, of which there are many—but more of these hereafter.

Let a wide border be made under the unsightly paling which you dislike so much; this, when covered with clematis honeysuckles, Virginian creeper, &c., and the border filled with roses and shrubs, you will not be displeased with, but like it, I hope, as much as the sides next to the shrubbery.

Having now disposed of the appearances in your garden with which you are dissatisfied, and directed you to make a border round three sides of it, I proceed to the fourth. I remember, you enter through the shrubbery on that side. At first, I hardly knew what to propose that you should do with it, because the trees that bound it are so large, that a border under them would be of little use; till I recollected the pleasure we all enjoyed, two years ago, in building an arbour, and my promise of making you a copy of the drawing my eldest sister made of us whilst at our work, (which I will send in my next letter.) Our arbour is now covered with creepers, the shrubs are grown large, and I have so much pleasure in seeing my sisters, when the weather is fine, bring their work or books, to amuse themselves in it while I am employed in my garden, that I strongly advise you to build one on that side, as near the trees as possible; particularly, as by planting a few evergreens round the seat, with some woodbines and trailing roses at the foot of the trees, you will soon have an arbour there. When I hear your determination on this point, I shall send plans and instructions for making this most useful ornament to your garden.

Thus, we have disposed of all the outside parts as follows:—first, the turf border, for the American shrubs;—secondly, the ugly paling mantled over with creepers, morning glory, roses, &c.;—thirdly, the south wall, covered with the more delicate and rare plants; and, lastly, on the shaded side, an arbour.

The middle of the garden, which is the most

difficult to arrange, is next to be considered. I am somewhat at a loss what to recommend you to take for a centre: I think either an oval or a lozenge, with little beds arranged round it, corresponding with its shape, best suited to a small garden; but I have lately seen one so very pretty, that I must describe it. The centre was in the form of a Maltese cross, round which a continuation of narrow beds, divided by walks, were placed; they continued the same pattern, the whole still forming the Maltese cross.

The best thing you can do, will be to draw on paper several designs, and then choose that which you like best, and think most suited to the situation; I have attempted to assist you in this, and send you two patterns. The dark parts are intended to represent the beds, and the white the gravel walks. I think I should recommend No. 1, as it will suit the shape of

LAYING OUT THE GROUND. 23

your garden better than the Maltese cross; besides, the latter, to have a very good effect, should be cut out on a lawn, or, at least, there should be grass walks. After you have determined on your plan, mark out the borders with

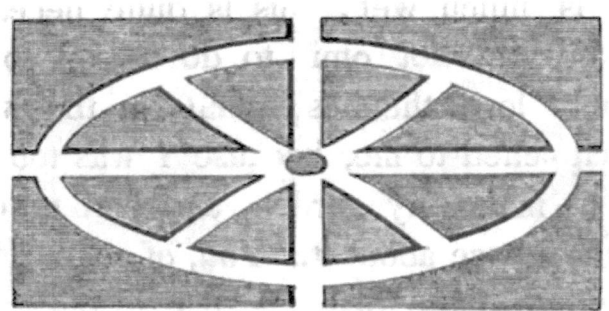

sticks, taking care that the smallest is at least two feet wide. The making these must be next attended to; and this must be done with great care and patience, or the labour of planting will be lost. As much depends on the soil, examine well the nature of yours: if it crumbles easily, and appears sandy, you need only dig and enrich it with decayed leaves; but if you have a clayey soil to contend with, as I have in my garden, you must dig out the earth to the depth of two feet, and put in a layer of brick rubbish, or coarse gravel and stones, the use of which is to drain off the water when there is much wet: this is quite necessary; therefore do not omit to do so, or you will probably lose the best plants in the winter: this happened to me, because I was too impatient to make my garden, and had no one to give me advice about it. You, of course, know, that most of the plants grown in our gardens come from foreign countries, from countries that are warmer than New England, and particularly from places where there is less rain and snow. If, during the winter, when the plants are in a dormant state, the roots are too much soaked with wet, they get mouldy, and rot, they are also more liable to be injured when it freezes, by the water which is in the root, becoming ice.

This draining of the borders is, therefore, the first thing to be considered; after which, fill them with a mixture of light loam, sand, and bog-earth, if you have it in sufficient quantity; if not, you must be contented with the loam, some sand, and a very small quantity of rotten leaves; you should let the borders remain untouched a few days, to allow the loose earth to settle, or sink down, before you plant the roots, &c.

As to the border for American plants, the soil should be entirely sandy or bog earth. As rhododendrons, the *magnolia glanca*, azaleas, and laurels, grow large, they should be planted at the back of the border, and not too closely together. I should say that rhododendrons should be at least five feet apart, or they will soon become crowded, and spoil each other: this crowding is the great mistake of all young gardeners. Always bear in mind, that in planting you must have "a prophetic eye," and look at what the garden *will be*, rather than what *it is*. The reason why the shrubs I have named are planted in bog earth is, because it is their natural soil,—the ground they grow in when wild. You will see that their roots are composed of a number of little fibres, not much thicker than hairs: peat soil being sandy, loose, and not clinging, and stiff like clay, is therefore best suited for their small roots to wander about in, and to collect nourishment from the earth; for, you may well suppose, that if they were planted in a clayey sort of earth, their fine roots could not penetrate through so stiff a mass.

As I have made it a point that you should not plant your shrubs too close, you may think the spaces between them will look bare and unfinished; in which case they may be filled up, in the spring, with stocks or other annuals or biennials. The *coreopsis*, or tick-seed sun flower, is a very showy plant, and will look well among your shrubs—the species *tinctoria*, native of Arkansaw, is very beautiful.

When the borders are filled, they should be edged, before you set about making the walks. Dutch box is the best plant to use for this purpose; though daisies, London pride, grass pinks, violets, and dwarf periwinkle, make a pretty edging, yet some of these lose their leaves, and some grow too rapidly for a small garden. The edging should be put down with great care. Nothing makes a garden appear more untidy than crooked lines; therefore do not spare your labour; and, to ensure the lines being straight, make use of a string, fastened to two sticks, stretched along the part you intend to plant. To make your walks, (which should be of gravel,) you must dig out of the earth, and this, if it be good for any thing, strew on the borders, to make them higher than the walks. They should be shelving on each side, to enable the water to run off. At the bottom of the walk, put about six inches of brick rubbish, and on this about six inches of gravel, throwing the coarser kind at the bottom. You will observe, that the drain to the walks will also serve as a drain to the borders, unless your soil, as I said before, be very clayey. After laying a coating of fine gravel at the top, and making the walks a little rounded, to allow the water to flow to the sides, they should be rolled. I ought to have told you before to make them wide enough to admit the roller, or you will not like their appearance in wet weather. I tell you much of what the gardener will perhaps assist you in; but I think it right that you should know the reasons why these things are done, in order to see that they are well done; besides, I hope you will find amusement in learning all these details. There are very few ready-made pleasures. I am sure my sisters feel far more delight in the nosegays they gather out of their own garden, with which they decorate the school-room, than the rich Miss Marsdens do in the magnificent productions of their papa's hot-houses. The gardener brings into their drawing-room the fine amaryllis, passion-flowers, and cactus, which he has raised with much trouble and at such cost; and after the young ladies have stared at them, wondered if they smell, and learned their price, they are thrown away, or forgotten.

My sister Jane has long cultivated her garden with great care: she knows the names, habits, and method of treating and raising all kinds of flowers; and, remembering the trouble she has had with them, likes them the more. She has undertaken the management of the flower garden, which, owing to my mother's delicate state of health, was much neglected last year; and I am enabled now, through her kindness, to send you a larger basket of roots, &c. than my own garden would have afforded. It contains some very good shrubs, herbaceous roots, creepers, and seeds of annuals.

Before I tell you what to do with the plants I send, as you are quite a beginner, I had better explain the difference between *shrubs, herbaceous plants, biennials,* and *annuals.*

The *shrub* is, in general, a low, woody, branching plant. Such are the rose, jasmine, rhododendron, lilac, honeysuckle, &c.; though there are many which grow to a great size, as the acacia, &c. These are again divided into *evergreen:* such are the laurels and *kalmias;* and *deciduous,* or those, of which the leaves fall off in the winter, and the stem survives; as, for instance, the lilac and laburnum. All these are propagated either by layers, cuttings, or suckers, and sometimes by seeds.

The root only of the *herbaceous* plant lives through the winter; the flower stem dies as soon as it has performed its duty, and is reproduced in the spring; such are the campanula, or bell flower, the sweet-william, and many others; and these are generally increased by dividing the roots, sometimes also by seeds and cuttings.

The *biennial* is a plant usually grown from seed, requiring, however, two years before it arrives at perfection and produces flowers, after which it dwindles away, and dies. Canterbury bells, foxgloves, &c. are biennials.

The name of an *annual*, denotes the shortness of its life: sweet peas, larkspurs, mignonette, poppies, &c., are annuals; they are all raised from seed, though many of the scarcer sorts might be grown from cuttings. As for the *creepers,* they are for the most part deciduous shrubs, requiring the support of sticks, or trellis; many annuals, as *Convolvulus major*, require the like support.

To return to the basket. It contains a plant of *Jasminum revolutum,* the flowers of which are yellow, large, and very fragrant; *Clematis Florida*, whose dirty white flowers appear at a distance like the passion-flower; and the scarlet flowered *Pyrus Japonica.* These are to be planted at the foot of your wall, and trained against it. I have sent them in pots, that you may wait till the season is more advanced, before you plant them out. You may plant, to run up a pole of your intended arbour, *Periploca Græca* follicle vine, which is an elegant, though not very showy climber. For the paling, I send plants of *Corchorus Japonica*, which will do well against it, and its bright yellow flowers will repay you soon for the trouble of planting, as they make their appearance very early. It is a native of China; and, though it stands the cold of our winter, it thrives best in a sheltered situation, particularly as it blossoms when the weather is very unfavourable. The Virginian creeper grows very fast; its principal beauty, however, is the bright scarlet hue of its leaves in the autumn. Among the prettiest American shrubs I can offer you, are the rhododendron, andromeda, the odoriferous kind, and kalmia. Plant in the rose and shrub border, the winter berry-tree, which is so called, because, in the winter, it is covered with bright scarlet berries:—this, I think, you will consider a very pretty shrub, and it helps well to make out a winter nosegay. Besides these, you will find in the basket, many common herbaceous plants for the other border; but as the names are marked on all, I must refer you to the gardener, if you require any particulars as to planting. In my next, I will give the necessary directions for sowing the seeds of annuals, and answer any inquiries you may make; as I shall expect to hear of the safe arrival of the basket.

Ever your sincere friend,
G

LETTER II.

February.

In planting shrubs and herbaceous roots, and in sowing patches of seeds, I must request you to pay great attention, *first*, as to the height they will attain when in flower; arranging them so that the dwarf sorts may be in front, and the taller at the back.

My beds usually consist of three or four rows of plants, each row nine inches apart:—in the front are planted pinks, violets, hepaticas, primroses, varieties of cowslip and oxlip, snowdrops, and crocuses; in the next are stocks, sweet-williams, some sorts of campanulas, and peonies, &c.; in the back rows, scarlet lychnis, poppies, monks-hood, splendid sage, and other tall growing plants.

FEBRUARY.

BUILDING THE ARBOUR.

Secondly, the colour of the flowers should be well considered, and great care taken to avoid placing two plants, whose flowers are of the same hue, together.

Thirdly, the time of their flowering should be attended to, and, in a mingled flower garden, contrive so to scatter them about, as to prevent one part of your border appearing without blossoms, while the rest is brilliant from the number of plants in bloom in it. All this cannot be managed in one year. Nothing but a little experience, and some care, will enable you to attain any thing like perfection in the arrangement of plants, as to size, colour, and time of flowering. The roots, or patches of seed, must be placed at distances equal to the space between the rows, namely, about nine inches; the plants are not to be placed immediately behind each other, but exactly half way betwixt, to allow of all being seen. But should there be a walk entirely round the bed, then the tallest plants, of course, must be placed in the centre.

Hitherto, I have said nothing about garden tools. It is absolutely necessary for you to have a small strong spade, a rake, a trowel, a watering-pot, a hoe, a birch broom, and a wheelbarrow of your own, in order that you may not be perpetually borrowing tools from the gardener, which are, besides, too heavy for you to use with pleasure. These you may buy by degrees; beginning with the three first, as being the most wanted.

I should recommend you to plant, about the middle of the next month, a few evergreen shrubs, such as rhododendrons, balsam fir, holly, and laurel, round the place where you intend to build your seat, or summer-house. These are all the shrubs of this description that I should think desirable for a small garden; and I must caution you against placing any one of them in the middle of the flower beds, as is usually done by young gardeners, who are not aware how soon they grow too large for the place in which they are planted, and shade the border; besides, in the summer, they have a very ugly, dingy look.

The only time at which evergreens appear to advantage is during the winter: even then they should be planted in large masses, and your garden is too small to allow of this being done.

Flowering shrubs, which have grown too luxuriant or straggling, should be cut and tied up, their suckers taken away, (which may be planted where they are most wanted, to fill up vacant spaces,) and the earth should be dug neatly about their roots. If, however, the shrubs are in a bed, in which there are herbaceous roots, it is better to use a fork than a spade, as it is less likely to injure the roots that have not yet appeared above ground.

You will find the new plants require pruning in a short time, particularly those which are of quick growth; on this point, perhaps, it will be better to consult the gardener. I doubt whether I could give you any good general rules for managing this part of the gardener's art: for there are some trees which do not bear pruning at all, such as the fir, larch, cypress, and cedar tribe; and on some plants the buds, which are in the spring to produce flowers, are formed on the old wood, as the shoots of the preceding year are called; such are the double-blossomed peach, the syringa, &c.; and thus you must be careful what you cut away.

In general, the best plan is to cut off all the straggling shoots, and to shorten them to about half the length you wish the plant to grow; as, whenever a tree has been cut, it will shoot out with greater vigour, provided it be in health; indeed, cutting a shrub entirely down is often resorted to, with success, when it appears to be dying, after all other means have failed to restore it to health.

Besides shortening the branches, you should observe if there be any cross branches, that rub against each other; in which case, one of them ought to be sacrificed; but, on these points, little can be learned except from experience. I shall, in a future letter, give a short account of the formation of the bloom and leaf buds.

Turf is generally laid about the first of April, but, from the size of your garden, I do not suppose any will be required. I ought to have mentioned, while I was writing on edgings, that a border of turf, six inches wide, cut very close, makes a very neat edging, but more labour and attention is required to keep it in order than box, and it does not answer well, except where the beds are very large, and the edges consist chiefly of straight lines: besides, the corners of turf are apt to be trodden down and worn out.

It is in March, that the seeds of auriculas and polyanthuses should be sown in boxes; but these and all the flowers usually called *florists' flowers*, (among which are carnations, tulips, anemonies, &c.) are so difficult of cultivation, that I advise a novice in gardening to be contented with possessing a few of the hardiest auriculas and handsomest polyanthuses in his borders, and not attempt to grow the finer sorts.

I shall begin the last of March, if the season is favourable, to sow, in patches, *hardy annuals*, which are to remain in the borders where they are sown; such as lupins, sweet-peas, candy-tuft, Virginian stock, and pink and yellow hawk-weed. In sowing these, I take away a little of the earth from the place where the seed is to be sown, and after making the place quite even, I sprinkle a little seed on it, cover it over with fine light mould: the seeds must be sown deeper in the earth, according to their size. Lupins and seeds of the same description ought to be put in separately: a ring with six lupins, planted three inches apart, will make a good patch.

The places where seeds are sown should always be marked by sticks, having the names of the plants on them; because, in sowing the second time, it is proper to know what is in the ground, that you may not put flowers of the same colour too near each other. The sticks are to be prepared in the following manner: some laths must be cut into pieces six inches long, and made pointed at one end, and smooth on one side of the other end, on which a small quantity of white paint is to be rubbed with a bit of flannel, as thinly as possible, and the names of the seeds written with a black-lead pencil, while the paint is wet. This process will effectually prevent the rain from effacing what is written on these markers. Herbaceous plants may be marked in the same manner, only that part of the stick which is put into the ground ought to be dipped in pitch, to prevent its decaying during the winter.

Yours very truly,
G

HELLEBORUS NIGER. *Christmas Rose.*

ERANTHIS HYEMALIS. *Winter Hellebore, or Aconite.*

LETTER III.

March.

I MUST now give a description of my *succession bed*, as I name the border into which I have collected all my Spring flowering bulbs. It is diamond shaped; at each corner are placed anemonies, and hepaticas, of the last of which I possess five varieties; the double and single blue, double and single pink, and single white; but as the single white is not very showy, and does not grow freely, I have not given it so distinguished a place as the others.

Entirely round this diamond, and close to the box edging, is a row of yellow aconite, the seed of which was sown last June; and next to that one of double snowdrops: then comes a row of the early crocuses, which are called *cloth of gold*, and which have the merit of opening when there is no sun, which is not the case with the other sorts: after these, there is a row of blue crocuses, then one of white; rows of the late flowering yellow and dark blue, follow.

Next to the crocuses, are three rows of hyacinths; and the middle is filled with early tulips, which, though not of the finest kinds, make a very good show when in blossom.

You are, perhaps, surprised at my possessing so many bulbs; I have but little money to spend in purchases, and as I think the greatest pleasure consists in raising plants one's-self, I did not buy these, or at least only a few; I have been some time collecting them.

The different sorts of crocuses, I have long had; and as they increase very rapidly, a good stock is soon obtained.

The hyacinths are those which have been forced in pots, and were given to me by the gardener, year after year, because they were too much exhausted to force again. I therefore planted them in good soil, that they might recover strength, after the unnatural way in which they had been treated.

The tulips were mostly offsets, obtained at different times, and which in two years become good flowering roots.

Opposite to this bed is one of the same size and shape, which I have filled with scarlet anemonies and blue hyacinths, or wild orchises, dug up from the woods and hedges. These two kinds flower together, and the colours contrast admirably; the idea was taken from a bed of red anemonies and dark blue hyacinths; but, as I was unable to buy the latter, I substituted the purple orchis which abounds in our woods. These borders are the pride of my summer garden.

In order that the anemonies should flower at the same time as the orchises, they should be planted at the end of October. The violets, snowdrops, crocuses, and hepaticas, are so very forward, that I expect they will be in bloom in April.

Since you have got some roots, and are determined on growing them, I shall copy from a book on gardening, the simplest method of making a suitable bed; but, as I said before, I do not recommend you, whilst a beginner, to cultivate what are termed *florists' flowers.* When you know more on the subject in general, if you feel inclined to grow carnations, ranunculuses, auriculas, &c., I should advise you to buy "Hogg on the Carnation," which is an amusing and very instructive little book.—

But to continue my instructions:—the bed for ranunculuses should be from eighteen inches to two feet deep, and not raised more than four inches above the level of the walks, in order to preserve the moisture more effectually.

At about five inches below the surface, should be placed a stratum of two-year old rotten cow-dung, mixed with earth, six or eight inches thick; but the earth above, where the roots are to be planted, should be perfectly free from dung, which would prove injurious rather than beneficial, if too near them.

The fibres will draw sufficient nourishment from it at the depth mentioned; but if the dung were placed deeper, it would not receive so much advantage from the action of the air, which is an object of consequence.

The surface of the bed should be raked perfectly flat, and the roots planted in rows, at the distance of about five inches from each other.

It is better to plant in shallow trenches, made nearly two inches deep, than to make holes for the reception of the roots. The making the holes hardens the surrounding earth, and the holes are sometimes not well filled up, and there is then an open cup left at the bottom, which holds the water, and not unfrequently causes the root to rot.

A little clean coarse sand should be sprinkled into the trenches, and the roots should be placed with the claws downwards, from three to four inches asunder, according to their size. When the trench has received the roots, it should be carefully filled up with the same earth that was taken out, so as to cover the root exactly one inch and a half. It is not usual to plant ranunculuses intended for show

(i. e. to blow in the greatest perfection,) after the middle of March.

I have, however, planted them in patches in the borders in April, and they flowered there very well; so that, if you think the preparing the bed too troublesome, you may put them in one of your shadiest borders, and you will have a good chance of their blowing tolerably well.

As it will require some time to get a good collection of herbaceous plants, you must be contented, this year, with annuals; and you will find that you can make your garden quite as gay with the commonest of these, as with many of the rarer sorts.

In order that the half-hardy annuals should blow early, it is usual, about this time, to sow them on a gentle hot-bed, or in pots placed near light, in a garden frame, or green-house;

but, unless you can transplant, or prick them out, as the gardeners say, into another frame, when they come up, or pot them, about four in a pot, and keep them in the frame, or greenhouse, till they can be safely planted out in the open borders in May, it is better to wait till the end of the month, or the beginning of April, before you sow the seeds of ten week stocks, Indian pinks, marvel of Peru, French and African marygolds, China asters, &c.

If you have no garden lights, you may, for the purpose of raising the half-hardy annuals, make a bed of a little hot dung, and put about three inches of mould on it. Before you sow the seeds, bend over it some hazel sticks, in the form of hoops, and throw a mat over the hoops, at night, to protect the seedlings from the frost, giving them the full benefit of light and sun in the daytime: but as this will be a troublesome operation, I should advise you, this year, to apply to the gardener for all the common half-hardy annuals, as he will, of course, have a hot-bed to grow them on.

I will send, in May, seedlings of the newest sorts of annuals, which have lately been introduced into this country. I have told you how to raise them, in case you wish to do so yourself.

While on the subject of sowing seeds, I must advise that, some time next month, a bed be sown with perennials and biennials, so as to have them ready to plant out in the autumn; the best are wallflowers, rose campions, sweet-williams, Canterbury bells, foxgloves, French honeysuckles, scabious and Chinese hollyhocks; the three latter will probably flower this year. When the plants make their appearance, the bed must be thinned out, and the seedlings, as soon as they have five or six leaves, should be planted in the places where they are to remain.

But beware of crowding your garden by planting too many, as they will all grow large and tall, except the wallflower. Consider also, when you plant out seedlings, the size they will be when full-grown, and allow sufficient space for them to attain that size, without injuring the plants that may be near them.

Our indigenous shrubs and evergreens may be planted soon, if required; they must be taken up with good balls of earth attached to the roots, that the smaller fibres may be disturbed and broken as little as possible. Continue also to transplant rose trees, and to take suckers from them, in order to make new plants; taking care, however, that the suckers have roots, otherwise, you will not succeed in removing them; or, at least, it will be long before they recover.

I hope to hear that you are better pleased with your garden than when I last heard from you, and that you think it will soon be as great an amusement to you, as mine is to, dear Harry,

Yours affectionately,
G.

LETTER IV.

April 6th.

You complain of the garden being dreary, and expect a flourishing account of mine. This is a bad sign: it seems that you are not contented with your own, and begin to covet that of your neighbour.

I am almost inclined to send you a long letter on this subject. Do you, then, suppose I have a secret method of flowering lilies and roses, in the open ground, in April? As your crocuses, hepaticas, and violets are in bloom, your garden must be nearly as gay as mine is; for, besides those I have named, I can only boast of a few anemonies, and snowdrops, and the yellow aconite.

The yellow aconite is one of the earliest of the spring flowers; it is very gay, and, if you can procure seeds, I almost recommend you to make an edging of it, by sowing a row quite close to your box. In May it will produce seeds, and the plant will lie down and remain at rest, till again, at the end of nine months, it is called into action by the early spring. This *aconite* (the common or popular name of which I do not know) is, I believe, a native of the countries where the snow lies long, and on the melting of which, the plant and flower come forth at once, and live through the short summer, awaiting to be buried again in snow.

It is singular, that variation of climate should not vary the habits of plants; but although plants that come from warm countries, are, by degrees, made to bear the cold of this climate, still, the alteration made in what may be termed the habits of the plant, is very small.

You will, I think, find this subject very interesting, when you know more about gardening, and grow in the open air some of those beautiful plants, which have, till very lately, been entirely confined to our stoves, and which are now successfully cultivated, during the summer, in our gardens.

You may now divide and plant the roots of any hardy herbaceous plants that are too large: this is, therefore, the season to ask for such roots as the gardener, or your friends, can spare.

I have been extremely busy since I last wrote, digging some borders which were neglected last autumn. I have had many herbaceous plants to divide and replant, and am now going to make a bed for some ranunculuses, which I have raised from seed. The spring-planted ranunculuses flower very late; they must, therefore, be planted in a shady border, as the sun, in July, is almost too powerful for them.

You may sow the following seeds in the course of this month, if the season is favourable: *mimulus lutea*, or monkey-flower, sweet peas, pink and yellow hawk-weed, flos adonis, larkspur, Venus' looking-glass, (the large sort, called *campanula pentagon*, is very handsome,) mignonette, convolvulus minor, stock, mallows, or any other hardy annuals.

By the middle of next month, begin to plant out any half-hardy annuals that are ready; or, if your soil is stiff, pot them, three or four in a pot, and keep them in a frame green-house, or sheltered with hoops and a mat at night, and turn them out after they have rooted well and begun to grow; by which means, they will not be so much checked by the change, as in transplanting them at once from the hot-bed into the open ground.

This reminds me that I ought to tell you, it is necessary to pay great attention to keeping the roots of plants, that are grown in pots, well drained; to effect which, a piece of broken pot, or tile, is placed over the hole at the bottom of the pot, and brick rubbish, broken small, should then be put in so as to fill up a fourth of it; but all this care is not necessary in potting annuals, which are, in the course of a few weeks, to be transplanted into the border. The broken brick, or tiles, at the bottom, secure the surplus water passing off through the hole at the bottom; if they were not placed there, the water mixing with the earth at the bottom would remain, and rot the roots of the plants.

OROBUS VERNUS. *Early Flowering Orobus, or Bitter Vetch.*

IRIS PERSICA. *Persian Iris.*

My garden promises to be gay very shortly: the hyacinths are beginning to burst; the violets, double primroses, (of which I have the common yellow, the purple, the white, and the crimson,) wallflowers, daffodils, and crown-imperials, are in flower; some other more tender plants, I expect, will blossom early next month. Among these are the common *Pulmonaria*, or lungwort, with its pretty variously coloured bells, some pink, some purple, and others dark blue; the Canada columbine, (rather a scarce plant,) *Fritillaria* of different kinds, *Orobus vernus*, (a small pink pea, to my taste, the prettiest early herbaceous flower we have,) and the beautiful Persian iris, which appears to some people to possess a perfume as sweet and powerful as the violet, while to others it is perfectly scentless. My *Sanguinaria Canadensis* will flower in the turf before the month is over: it is a plant I admire, as well on account of the leaf, as because all plants in blossom at this season of the year are valuable.

One of my greatest favourites is the heartsease, of which I have twelve very distinct varieties. I have planted an edging of these, by dividing the patches into separate plants, round a border I lately made for rock plants, in a very dull corner of my garden, where nothing grew before but dark brown trefoil.

With the aid of a few large stones, clinkers, and flints thrown carelessly about, and the intervals filled with fine mould, and planted with different sorts of dwarf cistus, houseleeks, periwinkle, the small variegated leaved sort of snapdragon, that you must have seen on old walls, and the last, not least in my estimation, the modest *Houstonia cærulea*, which our poets have celebrated,—I have made a very pretty addition to my borders, in a part of my garden that was formerly very ugly, and on that account always neglected.

It is usual for persons who have hyacinths and tulips to tie them up to short sticks, as soon as the flowers begin to be top-heavy. When you have a bed of fine hyacinths, you must protect them from sun, rain, and wind: the sun not only causes the blossoms to fade, but shortens the time of their continuance in perfection.

The rains and winds of this month are equally destructive: indeed, an April storm will sometimes strip off half the bells from the flower stalks, and snap in two some of the heaviest and finest blossoms; so if you wish to make a good show, and to double its duration, build a cover over them.

The great tulip and hyacinth fanciers have a

temporary awning for this purpose. The plan I have adopted is cheap, and is as follows. Get stakes four feet long; stick a row of them on each side of the bed, eighteen inches apart; drive them a foot into the ground, and tie rods between them, to reach across the bed, to support the awning. This awning may be made of any cheap material, such as coarse calico, or old canvass, or a mat thrown over will answer the same purpose; but care must be taken to remove this covering at all times, except during the full sunshine, or when there are driving winds or rains; if not, you will deprive the flowers of light; and as all vegetable colours depend on light, the blossoms, without it, will be pale; and the *instinct,* if I may so call it, of plants leading them to seek the light, its absence causes them to expend their strength in growing tall in search of more, and then they become what is termed *drawn.*

You will soon learn this property of plants; and observe that those grown in the shade are always both paler and taller than similar kinds grown where the light is admitted freely, and that the colours of plants, particularly the green, depend on light, and light only. This may soon be proved by putting a pot over any growing plant, and you will find that it will lose its green colour; but that when the light is again admitted, it recovers it.

Hence the common process of blanching or whitening endive for the table, by tying up the plant with bass, so that the light is shut out from the inner leaves, the putting pots over sea-kale, and covering up celery with earth: all of which, being deprived of light, soon become white.

Among the tender annuals, which should now be sown, are coxcombs, tricolours, globe amaranthus, ice plants, stramoniums, egg plants, and balsams. The three first named are too tender to be planted out in the borders, till very late in the season, when they are in flower, and should not therefore be sown by any one who has not a green-house or frame to grow them in, as they cannot safely be put out of doors till they are nearly full grown.

I should not advise you to have more than two or three egg plants, as they are more singular than showy: the purple variety is the handsomest. Datura stramonium is very handsome, but produces but few flowers.

You might sow some seed of balm of Gilead, or raise plants from cuttings: this is a perennial plant, very useful to plant out in May, as it grows freely. On account of the delightful fragrance of the leaf, it is very useful for the green part of a nosegay; and when dried, it continues highly aromatic, and is a great addition to a pot-pourri, or sweet-pot.

The green-house *Verbena* also may be grown out of doors for the same purpose: against a wall, it will live during the winter. I must tell you it is a deciduous plant, that you may not imagine it to be dead when you see it stripped of its leaves.

May is the month in which carnation seed ought to be sown. I have already said, that it is necessary to be what is called a florist, in order to grow these flowers in perfection; but, nevertheless, I have been so much amused by raising varieties of them, from seed sent to me from Berlin, (where they are celebrated for carnations,) that I cannot help giving a short account of my method of managing them. It is very simple.

The seed is sown at this season in pans, and

set near the light in the green-house, or in a frame, or even in the open air, if there is neither frame nor green-house. As soon as it comes up, the pans are taken out, and placed under an east wall, and sufficiently watered in dry weather. In June, the seedlings are planted in a bed of fine light mould, in rows, six inches apart, and kept well watered during dry weather. In the autumn, hoops are put over, (in the way I have already directed with respect to hyacinths,) in order that they may be covered over with mats in frosty or wet weather, the wet being quite as injurious as the frost. In the beginning of April following, every other one may be transplanted into the borders, and the rest left to flower in the bed.

In the course of the next month, I shall send a basket of plants with my letter, but I shall probably have so much of my spare time taken up with digging up the plants I send, naming and packing them with moss, that I shall not perhaps have time enough to write so long a letter as usual. As you desired to have two or three sketches of our garden, I have sent one; and you may expect to have one occasionally, when I have time to copy it; for I cannot yet draw from nature well enough to present you with any of my own.

Ever your affectionate friend,

G   G.

APRIL.

THE YOUNG GARDENERS.

LETTER V.

May.

You will receive with this letter a basket, containing some half-hardy annuals, and green-house plants. I also send a few roots of Dahlias, marvel of Peru, and *Commelina cœlestis*. These roots were taken out of the ground in the autumn, before the frost had set in; the earth was shaken from them, and they were placed on a shelf in the green-house during the winter.

You must treat them in the same manner, if you wish to preserve them for the next year: a closet or cellar, if not too damp, will do equally well. They may soon be planted in the ground; and if you want more Dahlias, or marvel of Peru, you must propagate them by taking off cuttings, with a small piece of the root, called the *tuber*, attached to each. These should be put into pots, and set in a frame, or greenhouse, till they have struck; or if you can crib a fortnight's birth for them, in a corner of a cucumber bed, they will strike root much quicker; and they may be sooner planted in the open ground, so as to flower this year. If, however, you strike them in a hot-bed, you must put them into the green-house, to harden, as it is called, that is, to make the change of temperature less violent before you plant them in the garden. If you took them out of the hot-bed, and put them immediately into the ground, the sudden and great change would almost kill them.

This treatment applies to all plants raised in the same manner. These cuttings will flower the first year, quite as well as the old plants;

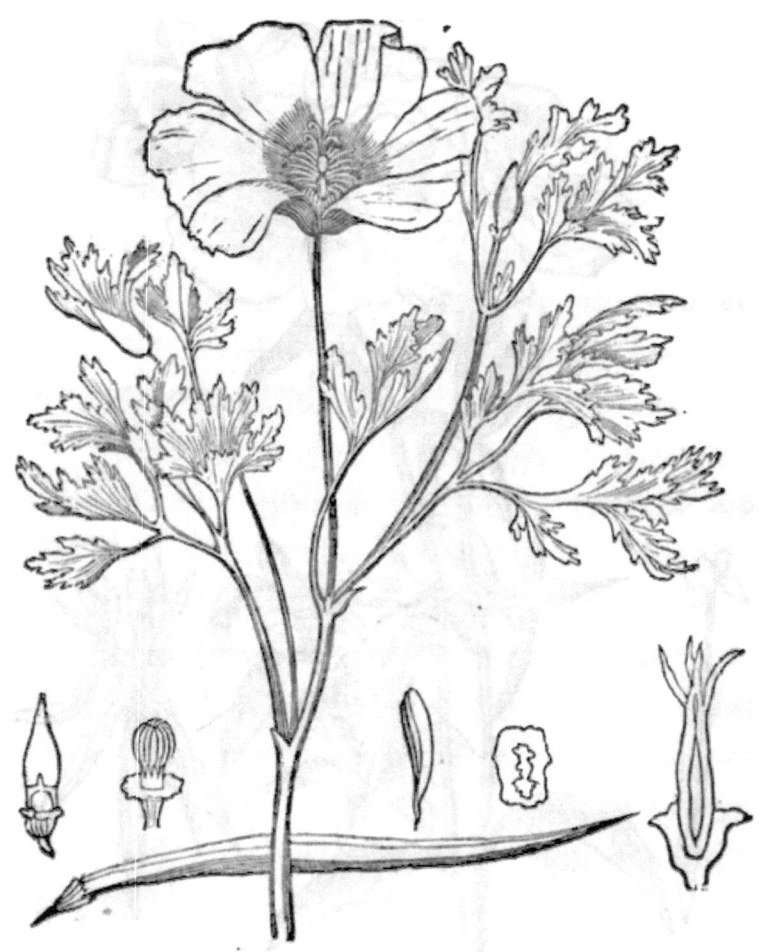

ESCHSCHOLTZIA CALIFORNICA. *Californian Eschscholtzia*

ŒNOTHERA LINDLEYANA. *Lindley's Œnothera.*

and I think you will find this the best month to take the cuttings.

Among the annuals I send, are three new sorts, of our own North American plants: pray give them the best places under your wall.

They are marked *Clarkia pulchella, Escholtzia Californica,* and *Ænothera Lindlyana. Escholtzia* cannot properly be called an annual, because its root, if taken up and kept during the winter in sand, will flower again when replanted in the spring; or it will live in a dry situation through the winter. Its beautiful deep chrome yellow flowers are not unlike those of the horned poppy, which I have seen on the sea-shore. I find that this plant sows itself so freely, that, wherever I have planted it, I have the next year had hundreds of young seedlings come up round the old plant.

There are many plants that are more easily

increased, by allowing the seed-pods to ripen and drop the seeds on the ground, than if they were gathered and sowed with the greatest care; when you find this the case, it is well, in the autumn, when the seed is nearly ripe, to rake the ground a little round the plant, and not to permit it to be disturbed till the seeds have come up. I believe the reason for these plants increasing spontaneously is, that the seed requires to be sown as soon as it is ripe.

I advise that you plant out the green-house plants which I have sent, in your warmest border, where they will flower far better than in pots: you must take cuttings from them, whenever you see any fit, which will be when the shoot has attained its full size. These cuttings must be kept in a green-house, or cold frame, during the winter. You will find it better, also, to take cuttings of those geraniums and green-

CLARKIA PULCHELLA. *Pretty Clarkia*

house plants which you plant out, than to take up the old plants, as they never, in my opinion, thrive when confined in pots, after being allowed to grow freely, which they do when planted in the borders; besides, the cuttings do not occupy half the space of the old plants.

The sorts I send are quite common; and should you not succeed with the cuttings, you will replace them, next year, at a trifling expense. The prettiest plant among them is *Calceolaria rugosa*, which will be covered all the summer with bright yellow flowers, which appear at first sight like little balls, till, on examining them, you see the reason why it is called *Calceolaria*, or slipper wort. You need not take cuttings of this plant till the autumn.

You will admire, also, the *Petunia nyctaginiflora*, which is very nearly allied to the tobacco plant, and is commonly called white tobacco.

You will find two kinds of *Penstemon*, (or beard-tongue) and *Lychnis coronaria*. The latter is a most splendid flower, and I should recommend its roots to be taken up in the autumn and potted, as it is an herbaceous plant, and cuttings of it may be struck, next spring, when it shoots up.

I think you will be pleased with the pretty purple *Verbena aubletia;* but the very eye of the packet is the *Verbena melindris.* Its bright, deep, rich scarlet, surpasses even the best geranium's colour: it grows as freely as grass: every slip you stick into a pot strikes root, and soon flowers. It will not stand the winter any more than the *Verbena aubletia;* so that you must plant some cuttings in pots in the month of August, and keep them in a greenhouse through the winter.

There is in the basket one plant, *Cheiranthus*

LYCHNIS CORONARIA. *Chinese Lychnis.*

tristis, or night-flowering stock, which, when you see it first open, you will wonder why I, who profess to grow showy flowers only, should have sent it, as its small, dirty looking blossom will not appear to have the least merit. You will smell it; and if it should happen to be morning when you do so, you will feel tempted to root it out as being both ugly and scentless; but have patience till the evening, and you will find its perfume as singular as it is delicious. It is one of the freest flowering plants I know, and will not leave off till killed by the frosts; and I think the more blossoms you gather, the more it produces.

This is not the only flower which emits no odour during the daytime, though it is the commonest of this description, and the sweetest, excepting always the pretty *Erinus lychnidea*, the scent of which resembles vanilla.

This, however, is a green-house plant, and is difficult to manage, being what gardeners call *miffy;* which means, that it suddenly dies, without any apparent cause; though I believe the cause to be too much water, and want of sufficiently well draining the pots, as I have before explained.

I planted out the only one I had, last year, in a warm border, after it had flowered in the spring; and it seemed to like the treatment very well, as it flowered again in July. It is not, I am sorry to say, so easy to raise from cuttings as most green-house plants.

As I have mentioned making cuttings several times in this letter, I ought to give a few directions on the subject. In the first place, all cuttings should be made with a sharp knife, exactly below any joint from whence leaves spring forth, as it is from these joints that the roots proceed. Next, you will find the wood of some plants, such as roses, &c., and, indeed, I believe, of most shrubs, requires to be what is termed ripe, that is, to have attained its full maturity, or growth, before it is fit for cuttings; while again, in others, as heaths, &c., it is impossible to strike cuttings from any thing but the young tender shoots.

I know no rule, by which I can tell you how to distinguish between those plants which require to have the cuttings taken from the old or from the young wood, except that if the wood, when mature, is very hard, it is found not possible to make it strike roots, except in a young state. These are exemplified in the case of heaths, where the wood is extremely hard; and in the case of roses, where it is soft and full of pith in the middle.

The pots, in which cuttings are to be struck,

must be well drained; and as many cuttings may be put in, quite close to the edge of the pot, as it will hold without crowding them, if they do not require being covered with a small glass, which is only necessary for cuttings of very tender plants, as heaths, or such as are made very early in the spring; in which case, they are put close together in the middle of the pot, and a small bell-glass, or a finger or water-glass, put over them.

Very little water need be given them, enough only to keep the cuttings alive, as more will cause them to rot. They require also to be shaded from the sun, and yet to have plenty of light; they ought to be potted off singly in small pots, as soon as they have taken root.

As almost all green-house plants will strike during the spring and summer months, it is not advisable to defer taking cuttings till the autumn; because, in most cases, the young plants would not be sufficiently established or rooted in the pots before winter; and they ought to be kept from growing during that season. Nothing weakens plants so much as growing when they should be at rest. This you must have noticed in the case of common flowers that are forced, or brought into flower early in the spring, which require a full year to recover their vigour.

While on the subject of propagating green-house plants, I must recommend to your notice a book,* which, when you can afford to buy it, and have acquired a little more experience, you will find very useful as a manual, particularly as it will inform you by name, how to strike each different plant; and is one of the few books that are of much use to a person

---

* Sweet's *Botanical Cultivator*.

generally fond of flowers. With this, and a little experience, you will soon become a tolerable gardener.

My tulips will soon be in full bloom and beauty. Besides jonquils, I have *Muscari moschatum*, or musk hyacinth, the flower of which is not pretty, but makes amends for its want of beauty by its fragrance. In the peat border, I have a beautiful and rare kind of *Uvularia*. The cinnamon and China roses are beginning to open. I have also some columbines, yellow alysson, and *Anemone pulsatilla*, or Pasque flower, an English plant, and very beautiful; besides several varieties of the *Anemone hortensis*, or scarlet anemone; of these last I have a whole row, and their scarlet heads look like a line of soldiers. I could name a few other plants, either in flower or just bursting; but I only know their Latin names, and I fear to tire you with a list of them.

You may, at this time, sow some of the half-hardy annuals in the open borders: they will flower late in the autumn, if the season be at all favourable. The best and most showy of these are Indian pinks, Marvel of Peru, French and African marygolds, *Chrysanthemum tricolor*, and *Persicaria*. Remember, however, that the Persicaria is a very tall plant. Put in also every month till July, where you have room, a few seeds of common annuals, and they will flower even as late as November.

I think that, what with weeding, raking, tying up flower stems, planting out what I have sent, and keeping them watered till the first shower, you will have more than enough to do, till I write again.

Yours very sincerely,
G.

LETTER VI.

June 2.

When I recommended that your garden should be laid out in the Dutch fashion, I forgot to remind you that *neatness* is the peculiar character of the Dutch, both in their gardens and houses. I hope this hint will not be thrown away, especially as you will soon find that sowing and planting are not the only employments of a gardener.

Weeds will soon begin to grow, and as it is only the sluggard who has weeds in his garden, I hope none are growing in your little patch. It would be a sure sign of idleness if any were found. In so small a garden, the weeds must be pulled up by the hand, as fast as they make their appearance.

I do not at all approve of hoeing in a flower garden. It may be done in a shrubbery, or where the borders are filled with coarse-growing herbaceous plants, or where they are so wide as to make it impossible to weed them without trampling down the earth. As soon as the beds are weeded, loosen the earth between the plants a little with a hoe, previously to raking the borders. Raking, however, requires some care, and will be better learned by watching a gardener perform this work, than by any instructions I can give.

When a border is well raked, it is perfectly even and smooth, and no scratches of the rake are left behind. I leave it to your own discretion as to how often it is necessary to weed and rake: the oftener this is done, of course the neater the garden will be.

I find, by always pulling up the weeds as fast

as they come through, although I have a large piece of ground to take care of, it is not necessary to weed and rake it, as regularly as it is to sweep it: this should be done once a week. After a shower, as soon as the gravel is sufficiently dry to prevent its sticking to the roller, the walks should always be rolled.

When the herbaceous flower stems begin to shoot up and appear to require support, they should be tied with twisted bass to sticks, of different length, according to the height the plant will attain; the bass being previously soaked in water, to make it tough.

Continue to sow both hardy and tender annuals, to keep up a succession of flowers. This is an important point to attend to: it will require some experience and forethought, to prevent your flowers from being so sown or planted, as to blow all at one time.

TAKING UP BULBS.

It will now be time for you to take up those bulbs, of which the leaves are nearly decayed. I can fix no particular day for this operation; because, as the bulbs flower at different seasons, so the leaves also will decay at different times; but the general rule is, to take them up carefully, as soon as the leaves have turned yellow, and to lay them under a south wall to dry and ripen; taking care to cover them with fine, dry, sandy earth, in layers, so that they may not touch each other. When the leaves are quite decayed, remove the bulbs, and spread them to dry under shelter of a greenhouse, or in a room; and, finally, after cleaning them from the dirt, take off their old coats, or skins, and put them away in bags, or drawers, in a cool, dry place, till they are wanted for replanting in the autumn. Do not fail to look at them, to see that they do not get damp and mouldy. If this happens, they will, most likely, rot.

I must here explain why bulbs are taken up every year: the great object is, in this, as in all other operations of gardening, to imitate nature: to make the existence of foreign plants, as near as can be what it is in their native place. Tulips, hyacinths, and most of those bulbs which are taken up, come from countries where the whole summer is dry, and in winter the ground is covered with snow; the spring rains alone call them into life and flower. Travellers describe whole regions in Persia as being covered in the spring with enamelled carpets of scilla (hyacinths,) tulips, and other bulbous plants: long drought succeeds the rains of spring, the leaves die away, and the plant rests again under the dry earth till the following spring.

As, in our country, they can have no dry earth to rest in during the summer, the best imitation of their natural state is to take up the bulb, and keep it dry; as it would otherwise be rotted by the summer rains, or caused to grow in the autumn; in which latter case, the plant would not flower in the spring, as the flower stalks would be killed by the wet and cold of winter, before, or soon after, it came to the surface.

There is another point on which I must guard you, namely; not to cut off the leaves of tulips, hyacinths, and other bulbs, whilst green. This is often done by ignorant gardeners; and the plant is thereby either killed, or injured for a long time. You will easily understand the reason of this; nature having provided that, in the very earliest of the spring, the plant should throw up its leaves, and, soon after, its flower stem: it has no time to lose.

When the spring goes, the rain for the year

is at an end; and there is, as we have just seen, no time for the formation of the flower and the roots in early spring. As soon, therefore, as the tulip or hyacinth has blown, new force is collected from the sap in the long green leaves, and the rudiments of the flower and leaf for the next year are formed in the heart of the root, where they lie dormant through the winter. If then you cut away the growing green leaves, you destroy the means of making the flower and leaves for the next year; and you might almost as well at once root up the plant. This applies to crocuses, lilies, &c.

You must not, therefore, in your taste for neatness, tear away any green leaves of bulbous roots, or your future prospects of bloom will be blighted. If you wish to be convinced by experiment, of what I tell you, (as, indeed, you should be, in all things relating to natural history,) you have only to cut in two a hyacinth root in July, and you will then see the rudiments of the leaves and flower already formed for the succeeding year.

But to return to my directions. I must advise you now to make pipings of pinks, if you can procure any good sorts, or to make some, at any rate, from your own; as these plants require to be renewed annually, in order to preserve their colours, and to procure fine flowers.

For this purpose, dig a bed of rich earth, half a foot deep, let it be the size of the hand-glass you intend to use, and sift the mould through a coarse sieve; press the mould firm, and set the hand-glass on the bed to make a mark, that you may not plant any of the pipings beyond where the edge of the glass comes; then take the slips from the plants, pare a little bit off at the hard end, and cut off a few of the bottom leaves: it is usual also to cut about half an inch from the top leaves; but, as I have shewn that plants receive nourishment from their leaves, the most scientific gardeners consider it wrong to do so.

After this, with a small pointed stick, prick them into the bed, about an inch apart; water them gently, but well; this settles the earth round the part in the ground, tightly. If this were not done, the air would get to the wounded part of the plant, dry up the juices, or sap, and prevent the formation of the new root. Then put on the hand-glass, so close that no air can get in; let them have strong sun heat, but no air till they begin to grow: water them plentifully, with a fine nose to your watering-pot, and they will strike quickly.

If you have more room under your hand-glass than you require, you may put in some cuttings of China and moss roses, or any other kinds of roses which will strike at the same time. Yet, if you have more than one hand-glass, it is better to keep the pinks separate. Carnation cuttings will strike in the same manner; and so will scarlet lychnis, double rockets, rose campions, double wall-flowers, sweet-williams, and Indian pinks. Slips of all these plants strike better than cuttings: by slips, I mean the small branches of the plants slipped or pulled off at the part where they spring from the main stems, or stronger branches; in all cases, a small piece should be cut off the hard end with a sharp knife, before the slip is put into the ground.

You will find much trouble now in keeping your garden as neat as a Dutchman's, unless you are very active in sticking and tying up such herbaceous and annual plants as require it; and in cutting off old flower stems and broken shoots. The sweet peas should have branching supports, and the convolvulus major long slender poles to twine round. You should now plant out the remainder of the tender annuals, or they will not have time to grow before the season forces them into flower: keep them well watered till they have taken root.

The Canterbury bells, rockets, and all the perennial and biennial plants, sown in the spring, which are for the next year's stock, should now be planted in beds, at about six inches from each other, till the autumn, when they may be transplanted into the borders.

Bulbs, lilies, colchicums, and autumn crocuses should be planted about the end of this month, to flower in the autumn. Do not confound the two latter, as they are different plants: the colchicum is often called *autumn crocus*, which it is not in reality. The stamens of the flower of the real autumn crocus, of which there are several varieties, produce saffron; the root of the colchicum is used in medicine.

You ought now to put in practice the instructions I gave you in my last letter, for making cuttings, as June is reckoned a good month for striking green-house plants.

Chrysanthemums may now be propagated in various ways: the most simple is, to take off a single stem, with some of the roots adhering to the bit pulled off: this method ensures success: the plants require only to be potted singly in small pots, watered, and placed in the shade till they have rooted; but it is considered, that cuttings make the handsomest plants, and produce most flowers: to make them, about five joints should be cut from the old plant, and set, either singly in thumb pots, or several in

JUNE

RUSTIC FLOWER STANDS.

larger pots: they must be put in a frame, or under a hand-glass, till they have struck, when they may be taken out, and transplanted into larger pots.

I have lately been employed in constructing a very pretty ornament for a corner of my garden; and as you may make one yourself with very little trouble, I will explain how I set about it.

The main part is merely a round, flat basket, in which some plants were sent from a nursery-man: this is set on four short stakes, with some crooked pieces of wood nailed on them, as rustic work, in the same way as the rustic seats and tables are made: these branches are fixed on, to prevent the four legs having a formal appearance: the inside is smeared with melted pitch, to prevent its rotting: this, however, may be dispensed with, as the basket is easily renewed: it is then filled with fine rich mould, and in it are plunged pots of all sorts of tender annuals and green-house plants.

I had previously made some holes in the sides of the basket, into which holes I introduced several trailing plants and creepers, which look extremely pretty; some peeping out covered with different coloured flowers; others twining round the wicker-work; and others hanging down, and in some places touching the ground. To manage this well, I found it necessary, when the basket was partly filled with mould, to open the wicker-work a little in places; and, after putting the plant inside, I drew it through the hole, leaving the roots only in the basket, which I then continued to fill with mould.

The plants I have put in it are, first, *Calceolaria rugosa*, of which I sent you a specimen;

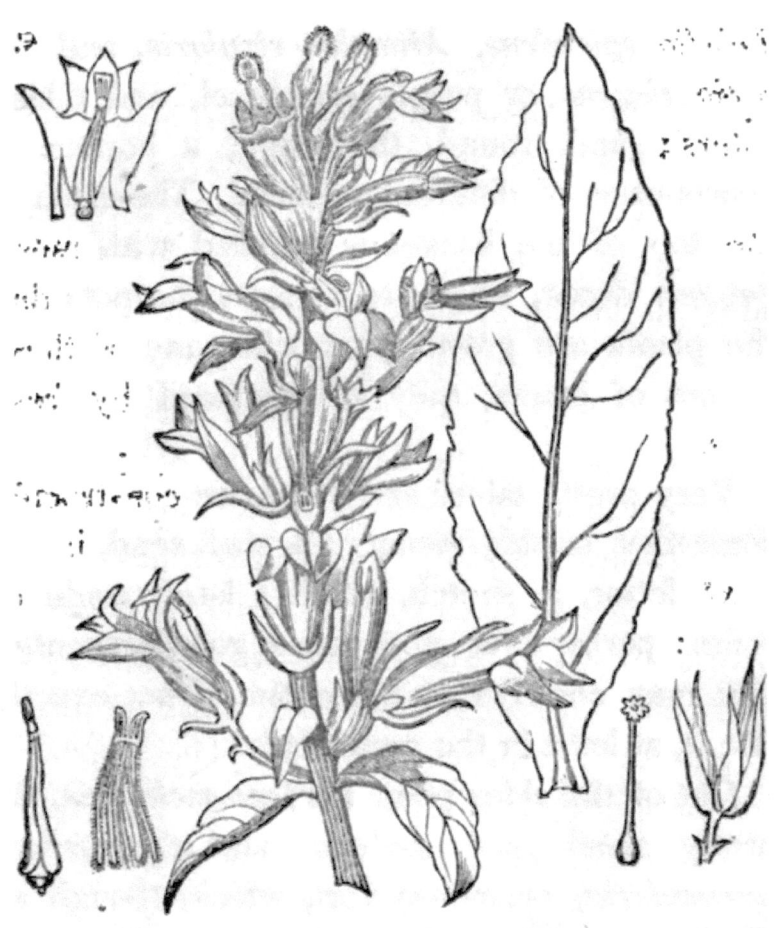

LOBELIA SIPHILITICA. *Blue American Lobelia.*

Lobelia splendens, *Mimulus rivularis*, and *Senecio elegans*, or purple groundsel, and China asters; and round the edge, a border of hearts-ease, of different colours. The earth at the top of the basket is covered with moss, pegged down, so as to conceal the pots that the plants are growing in: when any of these go out of bloom, they are replaced by fresh pots.

Very pretty tables and vases are constructed somewhat in this manner: I shall send, in my next letter, a sketch, which I lately made of some: perhaps, as you are a good carpenter, you may contrive to make one, if not exactly like it, at least in the same style.

Out of the sides peep *Verbena melindris*, the pretty small blue *Lobelia*, and the yellow *nummularia*, or moneywort, which, though an English weed, and found in any wet meadow,

MANAGEMENT OF CARNATIONS.

is not to be neglected, since, in damp shady places, where scarcely any other plant will grow, it creeps upon the ground, covering it entirely with its bright green leaves in the spring, and in the summer with its golden flowers, which are not unlike strings of gold eagles.

You see, I have been fully employed since I wrote; besides, I have had much work to do: my box edgings have been clipped, and my gravel has been weeded; this is very necessary, otherwise the seeds of the weeds, which spring through it, if allowed to ripen, would be scattered all over the garden.

I am now very busy tying up carnations; cutting off their small flower buds, in order that those left may blossom finer; and tying fine bass round those flower pods that are rather round than long, to prevent their bursting: and this I do to my fine pinks. I also slit the flower cup a little lengthwise, at every notch, to make it open evenly, and form a fine round flower. My garden now fully repays me for all my trouble: it is extremely gay, the roses are beginning to flower.

The *Phlox ovata*, the *Iris Germanica*, (or common blue iris,) the *Papaver Orientale*, (or fine scarlet herbaceous poppy,) the *Fumaria nobilis*, the *Geum coccineum*, (or avens,) a beautiful new plant, but now getting common; the double and single yellow Welsh poppy, and a very pretty blue flower, called *Lithospermum Orientale*, are among those in blossom at present, in my common borders, which I most admire.

The border is still more shewy than it was last month, as the azaleas and rhododendrons are in full bloom: there is, besides, in flower in it, a rare little plant, the *Rubus arcticus:* this plant bears a small pink flower, resembling that of the common blackberry, to which family it belongs; and though, in appearance, like a blackberry, it is very delicious to eat.

I had nearly ended my letter, without giving you a valuable piece of information, which is, that you must not fail to sow, in an eastern border, and in fine sifted mould, some Brompton stock seed, to have plants which will flower next spring; if you can put a hand-glass over the seeds till they come up, so much the better; after they are up, take off the glass.

I should have been sorry if I had forgotten this; because, next year, owing to my carelessness, you would have been without stock plants, for these are to be kept through the winter, to flower in the spring. I must not be so careless of your interests in future. I fear, I am often led away, by a desire to talk of my own garden, from subjects which are of more interest and consequence to yours.

Ever your sincere friend,
G.

JULY.

ARRANGING THE NOSEGAY.

LETTER VII.

July 7.

You are now, I suppose, enjoying the fruits of your industry, and your garden is brilliant with flowers. Without meaning to moralize in any great degree, on the subject of labour sweetening pleasure, I think what I have before written and so often told you, now comes convincingly on your mind. Until you had yourself reared plants, learned the means of doing so, saw when you failed, and found out the reason why you did so, the pleasure you enjoyed in the mere looking at a flower, when little else than its freshness, its scent, and its beauty, pleased, was very different from that which you now feel in regarding those which you have raised yourself.

I never meant to persuade you that gardening is the most important of occupations, nor that the lessons you are to learn from it are of such consequence, that nothing else is to be sought after; yet, as we must all have amusements, I think few will deny that gardening is one of the most rational. It conduces to health, gives pain to no living thing, and, without any very great exaggeration of its merit and praise, you may, by devoting your play hours to your garden, learn things that may be useful hereafter.

As I have got into a moralizing strain, let me impress on you the value of a habit of keeping all things neat, and in due order. The advantage of so doing will be considerable; the neglect of it must prove fatal, as well to your garden, as to whatever else you may engage in. I could write you a long letter on this subject; having myself experienced the value of this habit, it will give me pleasure to point out to you all its advantages, in the hope that you may be induced, even in early life, to adopt maxims of arrangement and order, both in thinking and acting.

You cannot hope to succeed in your garden, nor indeed in any other occupation, without reflection,—without really and fairly attending to whatever you undertake, or plan; and if you once acquire this habit with regard to your garden, it will extend to the rest of your duties and occupations. The consequences will be, facility of action, even under embarrassing circumstances; time always at your disposal; your mind free from anxious perplexities, such as beset persons who have no determined plan of action; and that respect and consideration in the world, which punctuality and decision of character never fail to command. But, lest you should begin to doubt whether I am writing a discourse on ethics, or an epistle on horticulture, I must return to your garden and to mine.

Among the gayest things which your garden boasts of, I suppose the common annuals, sown in the spring, are not the least showy. I know not what you may have besides these in flower; but, in addition to my roses, some of which are still in bloom, I have, among the herbaceous plants, *Phlox stolonifera* and *Phlox amœna*; *Spigelia Marylandica*, or pink root; the white, the blue, and the purple *Tradescantia Virginiana*, or spider wort; *Dianthus superbus*, whose pretty lilac flowers are deliciously sweet; *Campanula Carpatica*, which I consider one of the most splendid of a very handsome tribe of flowers, (the bell flowers,) *Hemerocallis cærulea*, Chinese day lily, *Anchusa Italica*, or

HEMEROCALLIS CÆRULEA. *Chinese Day Lily.*

buglos, *Lobelia siphilitica*, which is singular from its colour, and many others, too numerous for detail: all, however, making a mass of colour, and a show, which, I consider, puts me high among young gardeners.

It is in July, that I always lay such carnations as I wish to increase. I grow none that are very tender; but I have a great many showy border carnations, which I have raised chiefly from seed; these remain in the ground all the winter through. I have occasionally potted a few layers, to blow in pots; but they require such constant attention, that, unless you can devote much time to them, and have, besides, very fine varieties, they are not worth the trouble.

The manner in which you must set about making these layers is as follows: clean away all weeds and litter from the roots of the plants to be laid, and spread fine mould, about two inches thick, round them, that it may be ready for the young roots to grow in: have some small pegs, made from fern stalks, or small branches of trees; cut off a few leaves from the lower part of the shoot, and take about an inch off those at the top of it; then, with a very sharp knife, cut a slit half through the shoot between two joints, at about the middle of it, turning the sharp edge of the knife upwards; cut the slit through the first joint to the middle between it and the one above it; then make a hollow in the mould, bend down the cut part of the shoot, peg it to the ground with its head up, and cover the slit part with about half an inch of mould. You may lay as many shoots as you like, and as are fit, in this way; the only thing to be avoided, is taking such as have begun to send out side shoots, for they will not strike.

You will see the reason of this process: you create a wound at a joint; and where plants are wounded, many have a tendency to make roots when covered with earth: so far this process is the same as that which takes place in a cutting, except that the cutting is entirely separated from the parent plant.

There are some plants, however, which will not send out roots when entirely separated, yet will strike when a wound is made, and the communication and circulation are kept up with the parent plant. This is called propagating by layers.

In many cases, plants will strike both from cuttings and layers; but the latter are more certain, because of the communication between the old plant, which keeps alive the half separated cutting until it has formed new roots on the part divided; after which, the layer becomes a new plant, nourished from its own resources, and may be safely separated, either by transplanting to a bed, or by potting. This may be done in the autumn or in the spring.

If you do not understand these directions, or consider the operation of laying too troublesome, you may raise carnations by pipings, in the same manner as you would pinks; but they do not strike so freely as the layers, and the plants are much weaker, because they are longer in perfecting strong roots.

There are many varieties of carnations: florists have divided them into Picotees, Painted Ladies, Bizarres, and Flakes.

The flowers of the Picotees have a white or yellow ground, and their edges are fringed or jagged, and spotted with scarlet, red, purple, or other colours.

The petals, or leaves of the flowers, of the

Painted Ladies, are coloured on the upper side only, and white beneath.

The Bizarres are striped with three or more colours; while the Flakes are of two colours only.

The edges of the petals of all except the Picotees, to be perfect, should be round and smooth. Carnations with round pods are apt to burst: to prevent which, they should be tied round with a thin bit of bass, and slit a little at every notch, in the same manner as I directed with respect to pinks. It is usual also, to cut circular pieces of card, about two or three inches in diameter, with a hole in the middle, of the size of the bud, to receive the lower part of the petals, just below the notches of the cup: a slit is cut on one side, to allow the petals to expand as much as possible. This is put on before the flower opens.

You must pay great attention now to weeding, sweeping, tying up flower stems, and cutting down such as are out of bloom and decayed. No garden can appear neat, in which these little things are not attended to.

The seeds of some of your spring flowers are now ripe; therefore gather those you wish to save, and, after drying them in the air, clean them from dirt, and put them away in small bags, or packets: it is better not to take the seeds out of the seed pods, as they keep much better in them, (or, rather, do not dry too much;) but they should be picked from the stalks, otherwise they take up too much room.

My carnations now occupy the greatest part of my time: what with laying some, and attending to those that are coming into bloom, I am fully employed. The laying, you will find, is rather slow work as it must be done with great nicety.

While writing on the subject of carnations, I must tell you of a plan, adopted by a gentleman who is passionately fond of this flower, in order to shew, at any time of the year, specimens of the varieties he possesses. When they are in full bloom, he chooses from each the handsomest petal, and gums it down on the leaf of a blank book kept for this purpose; afterwards, he covers over the petal itself with gum, which preserves its colour; opposite to each petal is the name of the flower, or number of the pot, from which it was taken; so that when, at any season, he gives his friends cuttings or plants, he can shew them, at the same time, the kinds they are taken from.

You may still continue to raise all sorts of green-house plants from cuttings, likewise sweet-williams, pinks, &c., though it is better to do this earlier. The pinks and carnations, that have been raised from seed last year, will blow about this time; and such as are not worth preserving ought to be rooted up whilst you can distinguish them. Any shoots of the good ones, that are fit, may be laid.

I need not, I think, repeat every month my instructions concerning watering (in dry weather) those seedlings, or newly planted roots, that may require it. You will always be the best judge yourself of what absolutely wants water; and I need only caution you not to give too much, especially where the soil is strong, or close, as over watering will occasion the plants to grow too much, and thereby exhaust their strength in leaves; in which case the flowers will be but poor and few.

You must continue to take up such bulbous roots as have lost their leaves, and put them away till the time for replanting arrives.

Crown imperials, martagons, and red lilies, should not be long out of the ground, and may be moved now, if you wish to do so.

I think you must have seen and admired the standard rose-trees, which, of late years, it has been the fashion to plant in most flower gardens, on lawns, and even in shrubberies: they are themselves so formal that they are a great addition to a Dutch flower garden. As their price is rather high, it may not be amiss to inform you how they are made to grow in this manner; and as this is the season for budding roses, you may perhaps be tempted to try your skill.

The best mode of making standard roses is, to dig up some strong plants of the common rose, and cutting away all side shoots, leave one stem: this may be done early in the autumn, or in the summer, from the end of July till August. At about the height you desire your tree to be, you must insert in the stem, two or more buds of such roses as you wish to grow on the standard.

This operation of budding, which is very simple, consists in taking one of the buds when completely formed, together with a piece of the bark attached to it, and after cutting a slit in the bark of the standard, or stock, as it is termed, putting the bud into the slit. This is done by slightly raising up the bark on each side of the slit, then pressing the inserted bud down in the place of the bark you have raised, and tying a piece of wet bass round the stem, so as to keep the bud in its place, and exclude the air from the wound.

The circulation of the sap enters into the bud, just as it did into the bark of the parent stem; and, in the following spring, the bud will shoot out, in the same manner as the other buds of the plant. You must, however, cut away all the branches, except those in which you have inserted buds, and shorten the ends of these; you will have, in a short time, a large rose-tree, the stem of which is a common red rose, while the branches consist of shoots from the buds of all other sorts you have inserted. I do not hope that you can actually perform budding from this description: I have merely stated the general process. Ten minutes' practice, under the direction of a gardener, will enable you to perform the operation, which, though it requires care and neatness, is very simple.

I should here call your attention to the study of vegetable physiology; for, without some idea of this, you will not understand why the bud, so inserted, should grow, or why, having once discovered that it will grow, you may not insert a rose-bud into the bark of an oak, with an equal chance of success. This subject is absolutely necessary for you to understand, if you wish to become a good gardener, and to reap all the instruction and amusement which is to be derived from attending to your own garden. But it is too long for this present letter, and I must defer my intention to some other opportunity.

G.

LETTER VIII.

August 3.

I forgot, when writing on the subject of carnations, to remind you of the tree-carnation, which is a very desirable plant, and has the merit of being hardier, and of blowing longer, than any other variety. Planted and trained against a wall, it will begin to blow in June, and continue to do so sometimes even after the early frosts have set in; potted and put in a frame, it will flower till Christmas. Should you be able to obtain cuttings of this plant, they will strike under a hand-glass. I think you will have no difficulty in procuring them, as it is a flower the cottagers appear to be very fond of; for I often see it blossoming very finely against their houses.

Many of the poor, at least the most industrious and meritorious of the poor, are passionately fond of flowers; and I have always found them much pleased when asked for cuttings of any favourite plant. This I have no hesitation in doing, when I see they have enough; because I always have it in my power to make them some return, and because, also, I hope that noticing and admiring their little gardens, may induce them to continue so simple and innocent an amusement, and to pass those few hours which they can spare from labour, in the midst of their families, rather than in idleness or at the tavern.

It is remarked that those labourers whose employments are most sedentary, such as weavers, &c., are also more particularly fond of growing plants, and are, in fact, great florists. The Spitalfields weavers, it is said, have small gardens in the neighbourhood of Bethnal Green, where they cultivate auriculas, tulips, &c. The Manchester and Birmingham weavers are celebrated for their auriculas.

These flowers are, in many cases, a matter of profit as well as amusement to the cultivators. Florists have instituted societies, or meetings, at which they adjudge prizes to those who produce the finest flowers; they also sell at high prices any new and very fine variety they may have raised. Should you visit Lowell, our great manufacturing town, you will observe flower-pots in many of the factory windows, showing that the love of nature is cherished, in the midst of the din and dust.

I have so often spoken of florists, that I think I ought to explain what is meant by the word, lest you should confound it with the terms *gardener* and *botanist*, which have very different significations.

A *gardener* I define as one generally fond of, and conversant in gardening—who indiscriminately grows all plants which come in his way, and which his space and means allow him to cultivate.

A *florist* is one who confines his attention to the particular cultivation of some two or three plants; carnations, pinks, tulips, hyacinths, auriculas, and ranunculuses, are the principal flowers: and these are well selected, for three reasons: they are all beautiful; they all run into numerous varieties, so that every grower is continually raising something new; and they are flowers which improve, perhaps, more than any others, by great care and cultivation.

The same tulip, or auricula, grown one season, without more than the ordinary care of a general gardener, and grown the next with all the care bestowed by a professed florist, will

AUGUST.

GARDEN SPORTS.

be so different, that you can hardly imagine it to be the same.

Minute attention to the soil, to the time of planting, to the watering, to the shading, all conduce much to the improvement of the flower.

Dahlias and geraniums are now also beginning to be considered as florists' flowers, and they come very well within the class.

I do not advise you, however, to be a florist: there is but little variety in his garden: proverbially speaking, "his eggs are all in one basket:" the wire-worm, a swarm of earwigs, or a storm of hail, may destroy the hope and beauty of a whole year, at the moment when he expects to reap the reward of his care. Besides, a florist's views being confined, his notions of excellence become very refined, and often fantastical. Great importance is attached to the shape and colour of a flower, that has but little to do with its general beauty, and depends chiefly on its rarity: add to this, the best flowers of each class are often very dear, from their scarceness, and the great demand for them.

A *botanist*, again, is totally different from both a florist and gardener, though the two are often confounded by people who ought to know better than to use wrong terms. One of the Misses M. whom you may remember having seen here, said, the other day, while walking in my garden, that she was not aware I was a *florist;* and, in two minutes after, her mother praised the beauty of my pinks and roses, was glad to see I was such a good *botanist,* and wished her daughters might become equally learned: she was sure, it was not for want of books, for they had all the best books on botany at home.

Now, if the young ladies should ever take the trouble to grow pinks and roses, to please their mamma, and look into all their "best books on botany at home," I suspect they will find nothing about the matter in them. I hope, however, that you will be a botanist to a certain extent, as it adds much to the interest of gardening. Many of the best gardeners are botanists.

Botany is the science of distinguishing and classing plants, according to their peculiar characteristics; and affords the means of recognizing the marks whereby each individual species may be known from another. I cannot here enter into the whole scope of the science; you will find enough to satisfy you on the subject, if you look into one of the dictionaries or encyclopædias which you have at home. You will there see how important it is to be able to class and name plants with such certainty, that on seeing a plant you may discover, by its character, under what class it is arranged, and by what name it is called.

Consider, even in the case of these letters, what facilities this science has afforded. I have been able, in two words, to point out, with certainty, the plant I mean. I tell you the name of the family, or, I should call it, *genus*, to which a plant belongs—say, a *tulip*, which is the genus; and as there are many sorts of tulips, I add another name, which designates the particular sort of tulip. Now, by referring to any botanical book, which contains the description of the genus *tulip*, you will see whether the flower you fancy to be a tulip, agrees with it: if it does so, you have gained one step towards ascertaining the true name of your plant. But, as you find by your book that there are many sorts of tulips, you examine the plant, and read the descriptions of the different kinds, until you find one that corresponds with your flower, and then you have both genus and species.

Now, if this sort of character had not been applied to this particular plant, and I wanted to describe it to you, what difficulty should I have found in making you understand, by letter, that one I wished to describe! Try yourself to write such a description of a plant, as shall give every one who reads it a true notion of what you intend to speak of; distinguish it from all others in colour and shape, both of leaves, flower, mode, and time of growing.

The time which you would find that this would take, would be almost endless; besides, the talent and powers of remark which would be required, both in the describer and the reader, would be considerable.

Botany is a new science. In ancient times, there were no such divisions of plants, and, therefore, none or few of those described in the works of old authors, can be with any certainty known.

The mode of dividing plants into classes, is done by taking some particular parts of the flowers as characters, and all that answer in that respect, are ranged under the same class; thus you will find what are termed the *anthers*, always of the same number in a tulip, and this is made to form one of the signs, or marks, of the family; and it is by knowing thoroughly these signs, or marks, that a botanist is able at once to distinguish any flower.

Suppose, therefore, a person wishes to tell you all the flowers he finds growing on the Alps, and he sends you a list of three hundred names of the different genera, adding to the name of the family or genus of each, what is termed the *specific* name, to shew which particular kind belonging to the genus is intended. Thus, on half a page, he can tell with certainty, all the plants he wishes to describe; and although you do not yourself know them, yet, by referring to some botanical work, you are made acquainted with their history, habits, &c.; but if these means had not existed, what difficulties would there not have been in describing each particular plant! Indeed, nothing short of an actual picture would be sufficient.

I shall be glad to learn that you are not content with growing plants only, but determine to know them scientifically, and also their uses and properties. The first book on botany you look into will shew you how imperfect is my description of the science.

I have made a long digression, but, I trust,

not an uninteresting one. I now continue my directions concerning carnations.

If you have not laid as many as are wanted, or if those which are laid have not taken root, you may continue to lay them during the beginning of this month; but it is not advisable that this should be delayed till August, for, unless the weather be very favourable, these layers will not have time to make strong roots before winter comes. The stems of such as have done flowering should be cut off close to the roots, and the same may be done by the rooted layers which you intend to pot and keep in frames during the winter. After they are potted in fine, rich, light, vegetable mould, with a small quantity of loam, they must be set in a frame and watered. During the hot days, they ought to be shaded from the sun, and allowed no air till they have rooted, which you will know by their leaves becoming erect; after which, give them air, by degrees, till you can venture to take the glass quite off.

I have told you what to do, but it is not my practice to pot all my layers; though I generally keep a few carnations in pots, lest a very severe or wet winter should destroy those left out in the borders. I therefore take off half my layers when they have rooted, and set them in a bed as I do pinks, and protect them during the frosty and wet weather with hoops and a mat, in the same manner as I have before directed; the other half I leave on the parent plant, and in the spring transplant them into the borders.

You may lay Indian pinks, sweet-williams, or any plants of a like nature. Indian pinks, however, are rather tender, and do not so well stand a hard, or wet winter.

I have talked about shading weak plants from the sun, and excluding air from cuttings, &c., without, however, telling you the reason; and so far I have erred: for, when you learn the reason, you will know when you ought to do so.

The sun and air dry up the sap or moisture of plants, and if a plant be weak, (which it is when transplanted, because the roots, being disturbed, and many of the small fibres injured, it cannot exercise the office of collecting new sap or nourishment,) then the object is to save as much of the nourishment in the plant from being exhausted as possible, by keeping away the sun and air until it is in a state to furnish a full supply of sap.

The same observation applies to a cutting which has no roots: here it is material, except in the case of very freely striking or rooting plants, to keep all the sap in the plant until new roots are formed to supply it with more; and hence the reason of putting cuttings under a glass, which excludes the air; but, whenever the roots are formed, the glasses should be removed, as, by excluding the air, little sap is exhausted, the roots are not called on to supply much, and therefore do not grow; and the plant dwindles away.

Try this, and be convinced; one failure, with the cause of it found out, will often teach more than twenty successful experiments. Adversity and misfortune, in all things, are good, though hard mistresses.

If you have any wish to raise bulbous roots from seeds, these should now be sown in pots or boxes; but it will be so long before these seedlings come to perfection, even with great experience and care, that I should advise you to procure offsets of crown-imperials, martagon lilies, irises, and others of this description: pæonies, also, should be planted now.

I shall send, when I take them up, bulbs of the magnificent *Ferraria tigridia*, (tiger flower,) which I have succeeded in raising from seed so well, that I had this year a large bed of flowering plants of my own raising. Its flower is, in my opinion, the handsomest among the bulbous-rooted, but, unfortunately, it is also the shortest lived; though it compensates for this, in some measure, by producing daily, for nearly three months, new flowers. I shall send, also, one bulb of a very handsome yellow variety of this plant, which is called *Ferraria conchiflora*. I send, likewise, the *arethusa bulbosa;* it flowers in June, and has an elegant purple flower.

You may begin now to transplant and propagate most sorts of herbaceous roots, by dividing them, or by slipping off pieces of the plant, which may be either potted or planted in the borders. This work will depend, of course, on the state of the weather. Should there have been no rain, and the ground be hard and dry, it must be deferred to a fitter time, as also transplanting into the borders the seedling biennials and perennials which were sown in the spring.

When you transplant under a burning sun, before the plant can recover, the sun takes away the moisture, and the plant either dies, or is so long recovering, that the season passes away before it is able to produce its flowers. In case you should be unavoidably obliged to transplant in hot weather, shade the root with a garden pot, which should be taken off at night, that the plant may have the benefit of the dew. When a plant which is too large to be covered by a pot is transplanted, a deep basket will answer the purpose; indeed, small baskets are preferable to pots, and are manufactured for the purpose of covering plants, at the establishment for the education of the indigent blind.

I am now going to sow mignonette in pots, to keep in a cold frame through the winter. When the seedlings come up, I allow only four plants to each pot, and give them as much air as possible during the winter. After they have flowered in the spring, I cut them down, and turn them out in the borders, where they make good plants, and flower again sooner than the spring-sown seed. I am also busy collecting plants for the rock work, which I told you of. Among these, saxifrages are what I am most desirous of obtaining: now is the fit time to divide them.

My garden continues to be very gay; though

the first blaze has passed off. I have in flower three sorts of *Lobelia;* and, by the by, I ought to have told you to get a plant of each in the spring, as they are easily propagated by dividing the roots, either as soon as they have flowered, or in the spring: some of mine, in a turf border, are now four feet high. My *Salvia splendens,* (scarlet sage,) promises to be very fine shortly; and the *Amaryllis lutea* is flowering very well; but the China asters are at present the greatest attraction of my garden, as the dahlias have not yet opened sufficiently to shew all their beauty. I have many things, besides, among the herbaceous plants; such as *Asclepias tuberosa,* (or orange coloured swallowwort;) different varieties of *Phlox* and *Eupatorium;* and three sorts of *Liatris,* (gay feather,) viz: *spicata, squarrosa,* and *scariosa.* The geraniums, and other green-house plants, planted out in May, are flowering well, especially four varieties of *Chelone*, which I raised last year from cuttings; and am now going to strike cuttings of yellow Gerandia and *Orpine*, or live-for-ever, to keep through the winter.

I have written a longer letter than usual to-day, but it will be the last long letter you will receive from me on gardening, as I shall have, towards the close of the year, but few instructions to give.

Ever your affectionate friend,
G.

LETTER IX.

September.

I HAVE already said so much on the culture of carnations, that I fear I shall tire you; yet I must add, that if you have potted any layers, and they are already rooted, they should be taken out of the frame, and a small quantity of water given to them in dry weather. I have written more on carnations than on any flower, perhaps because I have myself raised so many showy, (though not what are considered valuable varieties,) that it has become my favourite flower: besides, I find the seedlings easily grown in borders. They flower at a time when the blaze of hardy annuals and roses is past, and before the most tender flowers begin to blossom; added to this, I think the perfume of the carnation nearly as delightful as that of the rose or the violet; the plants remain a long time in flower, and do not occupy much space.

I ought to have told you, in my last letter, to transplant the pipings of pinks when they have struck; this is easily known, because they begin to shoot up as soon as they have roots. I should not think they will be much hurt from being kept under the glass, if they have been allowed air since they began to grow: this you must not fail to do with all cuttings, before they are transplanted into the borders, or the sudden chill occasioned by removing them at once from the heat of the glass, added to the disturbing of their roots, would seriously injure them.

If you wish to have a bed of pinks next year, prepare one now of light mould, rake it smooth, tread it down, and plant the pipings in rows, five or six inches apart, and let the rows be at the same distance from each other. Next spring, take up every other plant, and put them where they may be required, in the borders.

It is not advisable to plant pipings at once in the borders, as on account of their small size, it is easier to water a bed of them, than to look for them among other plants, and they are therefore better attended to when together.

If you did not plant box edgings in the spring, the latter end of the present month will be the time when this should be done; and any edgings that have grown too thick, may be divided. Slip the box plants, (each piece having roots,) and plant them thick enough for the shoots to touch each other, so as to form an edging close enough to prevent the gravel getting into the borders. I have already told you how to ensure the edges being straight.

You must have found it necessary to redouble your attention and labour last month, in order to keep your garden neat; weeds at this season, as well as flowers, grow apace: there must also be added to the usual work of tying up, rolling, cutting off dead flower stems, raking borders, &c., the additional trouble of clearing them from the leaves of trees which may grow near, and which, if left on the beds, give them a very untidy look.

You must continue to collect seeds, and dry them as I before directed. Be particular in choosing a dry day for gathering them; for seeds are apt to decay, if put away in a damp state; from carelessness in this respect on the part of those who raise seeds for sale, great disappointment accrues to the purchaser. Some seeds require to be gathered before they are perfectly ripe; for when they come to full maturity, they burst their pods and are lost; for example, the balsam, which is called *impatient*, or *irritable*, from the seed flying out when the seed vessel is touched.

This property of the balsam is very striking, and is well worth your minute observation; it is one of the many and admirable means which Providence has taken for the dispersion of seeds, in order to continue the propagation of the species. You will observe the elastic spring which the seed vessel gives when touched; so as to throw the seed to some distance. This property is more remarkable in the wild English balsam, or *Noli me tangere;* and still more in the spurting cucumber, or *Elaterium*.

I shall not digress into an account of the different modes by which seeds are scattered:

you must have remarked those which have downy wings attached to them, as those of the thistle, which float in the air for miles; others are carried to great distances by birds, &c.

These subjects are amusing, nay more than merely amusing, they serve to display the wisdom of Providence in the creation; they show how great must He be who ordained and governed even these minute things; and how kind must He be who created all for our enjoyment and use.

I desired you in June, to sow some Brompton and Ten-week stocks: such plants as have shot forth half a dozen leaves may be potted, to be kept through the winter in a frame; a few may be pricked into the borders, to take the chance of living through the winter: if they do live, they will blow finer than those in the pots, though not so early. The pots must be well drained, as stocks do not thrive well if kept wet. About four of the Ten-weeks may be put into a large sized pot; but the Brompton stocks should be potted singly, to flower finely.

Like all other plants, they must be watered and shaded till the roots are established, and then treated in the same manner as the mignonette; allowing air whenever the weather will permit, or they will grow too tall, and the lower leaves will fall off: stocks merely require to be kept from frost and damp.

If you intend to increase the size of the shrub border, you ought now to get some fresh turf, and put it in a heap; turn it over occasionally, that all parts may be in turn exposed to the frost, which will cause it to fall to pieces; next spring it will be fit to use. Procure also some light loam for potting, or making new beds.

My dahlias are now in full bloom, though I cannot say they are as fine as I have had them in some seasons; this I attribute to the quantity of rain that has fallen this year: it was the same with the China asters; they, like all the tender annuals, grew so much after they were planted out, that they became too large and coarse, expended their strength in foliage, and flowered indifferently.

Besides many of the plants which I mentioned in my last as being in flower, I have now *Phlox pyramidalis*, *Aster amellus*, and the Carolina lily: these, added to the dahlias and a few hardy annuals sown late, keep up the reputation of my garden very well. Among the most delightful flowers in bloom, at this season, I consider the *Liatris elegans* (gay feather) to hold a high rank. There is a description of violet, the Russian, which is very valuable, since it flowers during many of the summer and autumn months. I wish we could obtain it.

I have lately seen a new method for preventing the pods of carnations from bursting, which I think superiour to the old one: it consists in cutting off both ends of a broad bean, and thrusting out the contents: the skin of the bean, which is remarkably tough, is then drawn over the pod of the carnation; there it dries, and its toughness prevents the carnation flower from splitting it. This plan is better than that of the card, which is unsightly.

We have turned what was formerly rather an ugly object on the lawn, into an additional ornament to the garden. You must remember the cherry-tree, under which we have so often sat and played together: for some years it has been dying, and the gardener wished much to cut it down. We resisted this, because this tree has always been called "the children's cherry-tree." Last year, I begged permission to make a border round it, and promised my mother, if I did not succeed in making it ornamental before the end of the present autumn, that we would no longer interfere to save it from being rooted up. In the border I planted, against the tree, variegated and evergreen ivy, and every kind of creeper that I could procure: my plan succeeded admirably; all have survived, and the tree is more than half covered with a luxuriant foliage, far superiour to what it naturally should possess. The multiflora rose, different sorts of clematis, cluster flowering glycine, and several other climbing plants, have successfully decked it with flowers. The Virginian creeper, *periploca,* and ivy, will be its best ornaments. I have also increased the width of the border, and filled it with varieties of hearts-ease.

 Your affectionate friend,   G.

LETTER X.

October.

I AM delighted to hear that you found my letters short; I infer from it, that our correspondence continues to be interesting. I have now so few general instructions to give, that I must confine myself to finding employment for you during the few weeks that you can yet work in the garden. I shall have scarcely any directions to give you for November and December; as, during these two months, I amuse myself in-doors with books, writing, and my other occupations, which I will not take up your time in relating, lest you should abandon your garden for some new amusement during the last month that it is possible to work in it, with any degree of pleasure.

I am now busily preparing a bed for my bulbs; this is a matter of great consequence! If gardening teaches you neatness, it may also teach you foresight; for as you sow, so you must reap; and if you do not provide in winter, your garden in the summer will be barren. The soil I use for the bulbs is composed of rich, light mould, sand, and rotten leaves. I plant with a round-ended dibble, the hyacinths and tulip roots in rows about five inches deep, and six inches apart; I put a little fine sand in each hole before I put in the bulb, over which I sprinkle a little more, and then cover it with between three and four inches of earth. Crocuses and snowdrops, of course, require to be planted closer and not so deep. The narcissus, I find, succeed best under a south wall: they should be planted as near the wall as possible, as the roots then receive less wet; and may therefore be left in the ground, where they will form fine patches. I have some planted in this manner, which appear to me to flower finer every year; in a bed, they should be planted four inches apart, and three or four deep.

Bulbs intended to flower in pots should be potted in good soil, such as I have described, and placed in a frame, or under a south wall, and then covered a foot deep with mould: this process occasions the bulb to throw out roots before the leaves begin to grow, and thus there is good support for the leaves and flowers; for it is from the roots that a portion of the nourishment is supplied: thus, by covering the bulb deeply with earth, the roots, which will grow at a temperature lower than the leaves, vegetate first. This is the mode in which the plant grows in its natural state; and as I have said before, the surest method of succeeding in growing flowers will be, as much as possible, to imitate nature.

The custom of planting bulbs at the top of the pot, and then putting them into a green-house, or warm room, effectually prevents them from flowering well, as it sets the leaves and the flower growing before there are sufficient roots to afford them support. When the leaves of the roots which have been buried have grown from two to four inches above the pot, they may be taken from the mould as they are wanted, and placed in a green-house, or in the window of a warm room, to flower. On taking the pots out of the mould, the leaves will be found of a sickly yellow colour.

I have already explained that the absence of light is the cause of this; placing them at a window in a strong light will soon restore them to their natural colour. This process of burying the bulbs, which I have just mentioned, is not much known to our gardeners; it is, however, the manner in which all the fine forced roots are grown by the London nurserymen.

I have told you that most of the bulbous-rooted plants are natives of dry climates, and are only watered by the spring rains: take care, therefore, that your bulbs do not have much water till they begin to grow strongly; and select a place to bury them in, where they will be sheltered from too much wet; though a small quantity will be necessary, when they begin to grow freely. The soil they are covered with should be light, so as to allow the rain to pass quickly through. While they are in flower, they may be well supplied with water. I told you to put sand round each root: this is to form a drain, because water is not retained by sand; it therefore prevents the wet from lodging round the roots, or in its coats.

You will observe that a tulip, when well grown, has a very hard skin: this should be carefully taken off before planting, (so as not to injure the rudiments of roots which you will perceive at the bottom;) the reason why this should be done, is, that the skin, when split by the frost, forms a sort of cup which holds water; hence the root, being held as it were in a basin of water before it begins to grow, is often destroyed by the rot.

Those who grow narcissus and hyacinth roots in glasses, should, after putting them in the glasses, place them in a cold cellar, to make the roots shoot at least three inches before the leaves, for the reason I have already given.

About the middle of the month, anemonies intended to flower early, should be planted in the same manner as I formerly directed as to ranunculuses, which may also be planted at the end of the month, or in the beginning of November, unless the soil be cold and wet; in which case, it is better to wait till the end of February, or beginning of March.

As the roots of ranunculuses and anemonies begin to swell as soon as they are put into the ground, and do not vegetate for some time, it will be necessary, if there is any sign of frosty weather, to cover the ground with straw; and if the frost be very severe, a mat must be thrown over the straw, but both mat and straw ought to be taken off as soon as the frost is gone.

The reason why this covering should be put on is, because the root swells from the addition of the water which it has soaked up, and as water freezes much more readily than the juices of the plant, the root is liable to be injured by the frost; and if once frozen before vegetation has commenced, it decays.

If the cuttings of the green-house plants have failed in striking, you ought now to take up the old plants, pot them, and place them in a green-house, or cold frame. By cold frame, I always mean one placed on the ground, without warm dung or tan; some ashes should be laid at the bottom and beaten down hard, which, in some measure, will prevent worms from getting into the pots. This I think the best manner of preserving all sorts of Alpine and hardy green-house plants through the winter, such as scarlet geraniums, chrysanthemums, aletriss, stocks, lobelias, &c. The latter sometimes survive the winter in the open ground; but, as a very hard or wet season might destroy them, a few roots ought always to be potted.

If the green-house or frame is too full to admit of your putting the old plants in either, you may adopt, for the geraniums, a plan I have seen practised with success, which is to strip off the leaves and roll the plants up in a piece of matting, and keep them in the cellar till the spring, when they may be potted and planted out again: they will require to be cut to a few shoots, or they will not make handsome plants.

The different species of geraniums may be increased in two ways, either by sowing the seeds or parting the roots. Where the first method is adopted, the seeds should be sown in the autumn, as soon as they have become perfectly ripened, either in pots or a shady border in the garden, where the mould is light and fine. As soon as the plants have acquired a few inches in growth, they should be pricked out into other pots, or beds of similar earth, at the distance of five or six inches in the latter case; but where this cannot be done, they may be permitted to remain until the following spring, and then be put out into other pots or borders, where they are to continue, being occasionally watered in a moderate manner.

In cases where the parting of the roots is practised, care should be taken not to divide them too much.

Continue to clear the borders of decayed annuals, &c.; to divide and transplant herbaceous plants, taking care to mark all roots with sticks, lest, in digging, they should be injured by the spade: in fact, I must advise you to leave no work of this kind undone, as there is always more general business to do in the spring than at this time of year. You may also cut back such flowering shrubs as have grown too large, as soon as they lose their leaves; put sticks to those that require it, taking care to suit the sticks to the size of the shrub, so that they may be seen as little as possible.

I think I have before warned you to take care, in pruning shrubs, to distinguish between those that form their blossom buds, at the end of the shoots which are to produce the flowers in the spring, and those which produce their flowers from the shoots, or any part of the stem. The lilac is an example of the former: the buds which are to blow in the spring, are made in the autumn, at the tips of the shoots; and if you take, in September, a full round bud of the lilac, you will see the little embryo flower and leaves formed ready for the next year. The rose is an example of the latter class: here the flowers are formed on the new spring shoots on any part of the stem, and it is therefore best to prune away, in the autumn, all the old shoots of the preceding year, down to two or three buds, from which the new shoots arise to produce flowers in the following summer.

Towards the end of the month, you may begin to transplant the following shrubs:—*Althea frutex, Daphne mezereon,* lilacs, syringas, honeysuckles, roses, jasmines, &c. But let this be done with care; and do not, to save a little trouble in digging, make the holes too small for the roots, which should all be carefully preserved, (unless the plant grows too luxuriantly,) and well spread out. If, however, the shrub grows too freely, then cut the roots short, this will check the growth for a year or two. Next see that you place the stem upright in the hole; and after having thrown in a little earth, shake the tree, that the mould may settle about the roots, and tread it over to keep the plant steady.

When planting roses, endeavour to obtain suckers of one called the Chinese ever blooming rose; it will help admirably to cover the paling, as it is a trailing rose. I have planted it against a shed, which I have covered with ivy and other creepers: it grows very fast, and flowers very early. Mine has been planted three years; and, last year, it made one shoot, or sucker, which was at least fifteen feet in length; this branched out on both sides, and, early in June, was covered with blossoms: this year, also, it has made a great many very strong suckers.

You must water the carnations, and all plants that are in the cold frame, during the winter; but this must be done with great care and discretion. I have before observed, plants are more likely to die from damp and water soaking in the pots, than from cold. They ought now to have the glasses put on the frames every night; but, during the day, they should have plenty of air.

The frosts have not yet injured the dahlias;

they are now almost the only ornament of the garden: the stocks, mignonette, and some *Œnotheras*, still exist, but they have nearly lost both smell and colour. Some green-house plants, which I turned out under a wall, are still lingering in flower : *Calceolaria rugosa;* night-scented stocks, and *Plumbago capensis,* (formerly considered a hot-house plant,) are among the number.

You will receive, with this letter, the last basket of plants that I shall send this year; and with it a drawing of a Roman arbour, which was made from one discovered in the ruins of Pompeii; and which, in our love for classical ornament, we mean, with the assistance of my brother, to imitate at the end of our garden. I must say, however, the seats which the Romans used for reclining on, do not appear to be either pleasant or convenient.

OCTOBER.

A ROMAN ARBOUR.

LETTER XI.

November.

My instructions for the present month will occupy but a short space; though, perhaps, you will employ some time in fulfilling them. I know but little to be done during this month, except digging the borders, and laying them up rough and hollow, for the winter. Before beginning to do this, pull up all the annuals; then trim round such roots as have grown too large, as your plants should never be allowed to get too big for the size of your garden.

Prune such shrubs as require it; this you will not do to azaleas and rhododendrons, nor to any shrubs that have already formed their bloom buds for the next year. Go round, and put markers and sticks to such roots as require them, and take away the sticks of those from which you have cut away the flower stems. If the sticks be still sound, clean them, tie them up in bundles, and put them away with the tools; this will save some labour next year, as there will be fewer to cut. Take off suckers where they are not wanted, and give them away, or plant them deep in the ground all together till the spring; this, in gardeners' language, is called "laying them by the heels:" perhaps you may then find some use for them.

After having done all this, turn over the borders with a small spade, or a fork, if you have one, unless the soil be very light. The dead leaves may be dug in, and buried deep in the borders, as they are of great use in manuring and lightening the soil; but if the soil be much exhausted or worn out, from having been long cultivated without any manure, you will do well to dig in some very rotten dung, or an additional quantity of decayed leaves; though, in general, it is best not to add much manure; the flower borders are not to be raked after this digging, but left rough all the winter, that the frosts may break the ground and make it crumble.

The tulips and ranunculus roots should be planted about the middle of the month: the hyacinths, I presume, were put in the ground in October. The London tulip fanciers usually plant their bulbs on or about the Lord Mayor's day. You will say this is rather a cockney time to fix on. Remember to protect them as well as the anemonies, hyacinths, and ranunculuses, from heavy rains, as well as from frosts; especially from frosts coming after much rain, when the roots are much saturated with wet. Should the winter be very severe, you must put a little straw over them

You ought now to collect a heap of leaves to rot into mould for next year; and your turf and loam heaps should be turned and broken occasionally. The gravel walks should be swept and rolled every week during the winter, even when there is no work to be done in the garden: and indeed, I think you will find this no bad exercise in cold weather.

Do not forget to pay great attention to the beds of carnations; they must be protected from both frost and wet. And, I may here mention again, that the great object with respect to most of our garden plants, like carnations, &c., is to guard against too much wet; this is far more injurious than frost: many of the plants in our gardens are killed by the effects of wet more than by the frost.

This observation applies particularly to Alpine plants, or those that come from mountainous countries, which are covered all through the winter with snow. You will be surprised to find that a plant which, in its native country, lives well through an eight months' winter, under a coat of snow, dies and dwindles away during our far milder climate.

I must try to explain this, as well as I can; and if I succeed, it will be of great advantage in two ways: first, it will give you a habit of thinking, and of looking into the reason of things, and will teach you not to remain in silly wonder at what you cannot understand; secondly, it will give you the best chance of growing Alpines, which are my favourite plants; so, indeed, they must be with all who have small gardens; as they are generally dwarfs, and very beautiful; moreover, nearly all of them are amongst our earliest harbingers of spring.

I must, however, make you a bit of a philosopher, to enable you to understand me. Some bodies retain heat longer than others, and snow is one of these bodies: different substances are said to be good or bad conducters of heat, in proportion to their capacity of keeping or losing it. Air is a body, marble is a body, and water is a body; but when marble and water are surrounded by air, you find the air is warm, in comparison with water and marble.

Now, if these bodies retained heat in the same degree as the air which surrounds them, their temperature would be the same; yet you find the water and marble colder than the air; that is, the marble and the water part with some of the heat to the air, which therefore has more of it, and is consequently warmer: now, snow does not part with heat quickly; that is, it does not become cold quickly, which is the same thing; and when it has formed a covering to the earth, and the external air is colder than the snow, the snow retains, in a great degree, its heat, and prevents the external air from communicating its cold to the earth beneath; so that plants under snow are thus, in a great measure, prevented from experiencing the intense cold of the external air; in other words, they are not colder than the snow itself, whilst, however, the air is far colder.

In this country we have often intense cold, and no thick coating of snow to cover the plants, which are consequently left exposed, and are killed by it. In addition, the rains of our autumns and winters soak into the ground, and into the heart of the plant; and as the principle or power of life is very weak during the winter, the plant being in a dormant state, cannot resist the effect of the water, which rots it, beginning first with the leaves, which die on the approach of winter; and the disease, or rot, is continued from the dead to the living part.

Again, in the Alps, the plant, under the snow, is prevented from growing till the snow melts and the warm winds come; but in our climate, it happens often in the winter, and in the early part of spring, that a few fine days will cause the plant to grow before its time; then frosts return, check, and sometimes even kill the opening buds, which were reserved for the great effort of nature to be made in spring; the consequence is, that the plant either dies, or lingers in a poor miserable state of existence, scarcely able to make leaves again to keep it alive, far less to throw up flowers. Yet the same plant, in its native Alps, secure under its snow mantle, reposes throughout the cold, till warmed by the sun, which at once melts the snow and calls it into life and bloom in a few days, without the fear of those chilling chances which our uncertain climate dooms it to experience.

Without being a great traveller, I have seen the effect of an Alpine spring. In May, all is one mass of white snow, silence, and desolation. The power of the sun, with the coming year, at once turns the white to green, and in a few days, whole rocks, whole districts, I may say, are covered with white and yellow saxifrages, different sorts of violets, primulas, and blue gentians; and the little trailing strawberry clings to the sides of endless ranges of towering rocks: this change, effected in so short a time, appears more like enchantment than the slow and uncertain return of spring to which we are accustomed.

I do not write all this to put you out of humour with our spring: it has, like that of the

Alps, its beauties: the fine sunny days coming at intervals, a soft air, after the drying March winds, the cheerfulness of the birds, and the struggling plants venturing forth, (often too boldly,) are perhaps as pleasing, from the variety and the uncertainty, as the sudden and certain change I have attempted to describe.

You will see by what I have said, that, if you grow Alpine plants, you must imitate, as far as possible, an Alpine climate; and, as you have no certainty of allowing six months of snowy jackets for the natives of snowclad hills, you must discover a substitute for it: this will best be found in a frame, in which the most tender of these plants may be preserved during the winter. Care must be taken that the pots be well drained; and a mat should be thrown over the frames during very frosty weather.

The more hardy Alpine plants, which are left

out all the winter, should be planted high above the ground, on rock work, that the wet may drain off, and these, as well as such as are in pots, should not have a southern aspect, lest they be too early and treacherously coaxed into vegetation. This treatment is absolutely necessary to preserve all the primula tribe, among which the auricula, (the most beautiful of florists' flowers,) is classed.

I had almost forgotten the dahlias: I am about to take up mine, their leaves being destroyed by the frost three nights ago. I find I am more fortunate than some of my friends, whose dahlias were touched by the frost in the middle of last month. I shall now take them, cut off the stems close to the roots, and put them away in a dry place, secure from cold and damp till the spring.

The same must be done by the roots of mar-

ARGEMONE GRANDIFLORA. *Large-flowered Mexican Poppy.*

vel of Peru and *Commelina cœlestis.* If, however, the soil be dry, the roots of dahlias may be left in the ground all the winter, taking care to put a shovel full of rotten leaves, or very rotten dung, over the crown of each root. This is not, however, quite safe, as the frost or wet sometimes destroys them.

The few plants that continue to flower are very shabby, though (till my dahlias were destroyed) I could gather a handsome nosegay for the library twice a week; I have now only an *Argemone grandiflora, Dianthus superbus,* the white tobacco, double white chamomile, yellow fumaria, a few asters, and some stocks, to boast of; and the flowers of these are so pale, and the plants have grown so tall and straggling, that they are scarcely ornamental: yet, as I feel that till the chrysanthemums blow, they are all I am to have this year, I cannot make up my mind to pull them up.

I must now conclude, in order that we may both profit by the few tolerably dry days that we may have this month, to put our gardens in proper order against the winter.

Ever yours sincerely,
G

LETTER XII.

December 3.

I HAVE really so little to add to my directions for the last month, on the subject of the garden, that, as we are to meet soon, I should not have written again, had you not especially desired that I should send one more letter on the subject, to add to the eleven I have already sent. I am well pleased by the care you have taken of these, and I hope they will be useful as a gardening manual. I recommend, however, that you should, from time to time, add your own observations, and the results of your experience to them. If this be done with care, you will soon obtain a valuable stock of information.

My principal object has been to call your attention, generally, to the subject of gardening and botany; and I shall have succeeded in my object, if I induce you to think on the subject; you must, however, seek elsewhere for more detailed instruction.

If you should pay some attention to vegetable physiology, I think you would derive much amusement from merely seeing and understanding the reason of the different operations that are daily taking place in a garden.

Vegetable physiology is not, like botany, a mere classification of plants, and determination of their names: it is the science which makes one acquainted with their internal and external structure, their nature, habits, properties, manner of growing, and the functions, or duties, of their different organs: we learn from it, how the hard and apparently dry seed, on being placed in the ground, begins to germinate, or bud forth; and the reason why this process takes place under ground only, when the seed is almost entirely deprived of light and air, which are, you already know, essentially necessary to the health of that portion of the plant which is above ground. You will trace the seed from the first period of its existence, in the bosom of the flower, through its various stages, till it becomes an individual, separate plant.

After becoming acquainted with the natural organs of plants, you will see how the sap, (originally merely water, containing different crude materials dissolved in it,) absorbed by the roots, the extremities of which, for that purpose, resemble little sponges, rises, every spring, through the wood of the trees, and is conveyed to the bud, which it developes, and to the leaves, in which the evaporation of the useless particles takes place, through pores furnished for that purpose. You will follow it in its descent through the bark, depositing, in its progress, all the nourishing particles it contains, and thereby increasing the tree in size and height.

The examination of the flower, the different modes in which the fruit is formed, and the peculiar secretions of plants, (such as oils, gums, resin, milk, &c.,) cannot, I think, fail to interest.

Vegetable physiology is most pleasing, perhaps, to those acquainted in some degree with the physiology of animals; because they are able to compare the organs, growth, &c., of both animal and vegetable kingdoms. It must be regarded as an important science, if we merely consider the direct benefits we derive from some plants in nourishment for ourselves, and many of the animals necessary to our existence; and relief from sickness, by the medicinal properties of others.

Again, a close investigation of the structure, habits, and diseases of plants, will not only enable us to distinguish such as are suited to our climate, but, being intimately connected with agriculture, will teach us how to administer to the well being of those we already cultivate, and thereby improve them, as well as to supply, artificially, those advantages which they possess, naturally, in their own countries.

I have several times, I think, in my letters, alluded to the usefulness of gardening, as an amusement, in inculcating a love of industry, order, and neatness: but I trust you will forgive my repeating what I remember to have said before, that I never wished to persuade you that it is the most important of occupations.

I could quote what many great, and, what is more, many good men have said with respect to gardening, as an amusement fitted for good men. I shall, when I see you, relate some stories of the love of great men for the pursuit itself. One of the wisest that ever lived in England,—I mean Lord Bacon,—pursued gardening with eagerness and delight, and in its pursuit made some of the experiments, and acquired that habit of examination, which has made him celebrated in every age.

We have not yet, in our country, paid that attention to gardening, generally, which the beauty of flowers and the benefits resulting to the cultivator demand. But our Horticultural Societies, by their exhibitions, are doing much to awaken public attention, and it cannot be a long time before the pleasures of the garden and green-house will be fully appreciated by our citizens.

You tell me, you continue so fond of the garden, that you will brave the cold, during

December, to work in it; but there is little to be done if you have finished digging, besides keeping it swept and rolled. The frame plants, however, must be attended to; they must have air, when the weather is mild, and be protected with mats from the frosts. I have before said, that, though the frost is to be kept from the frames, the plants must not be allowed to grow, with the exception of a few, to which it is natural to vegetate at this season: among these is the *Calceolaria*. When you find any plant beginning to grow, or *draw*, as it is termed, you may be certain that you are treating it too tenderly, and must alter your management, allowing it, by degrees, more air. I have already explained, in a preceding letter, the reason of this.

I therefore now take my leave of the subject on which we have been corresponding, regretting that I have not been able to give more information, yet pleased to find that I have been of some use to you.

Consider me ever as - -
     Your affectionate friend,
         G.

INDEX.

A.

Aconite, Winter or Yellow 59
Ænothera Lindlyana . 79
Alpine plants 181—186.—Directions for their management 86
Alpine Spring, contrasted with the spring in America 185
Amaryllis lutea . . . 151
American shrubs 18. 21.—Directions respecting 25. 54
Anchusa Italica . . . 118
Anchusa sempervirens 118
Anemone hortensis, or Scarlet Anemone . . . 89
Anemone pulsatilla, or Pasque flower 89
Anemonies 49. 89.—Time for planting 168.—Instructions respecting . . 169. 180

Annuals, general directions for . 32, 33. 53. 62. 91
Annuals, hardy 43. 53. 91
Annuals, half-hardy 53. 91
Annuals, tender 69. 89. 99
Arbour for a Garden . 20
Argemone Grandiflora, or large flowered Mexican Poppy 190
Arrangement of plants in beds 35
Artisans mostly florists 133
Asclepias tuberosa . . 151
Aster amellus . . . 160
Auriculas, sowing seed of 42
Awning, a cheap, for bulbous plants in flower . . 68
Azaleas 25.—Time of blooming 110

INDEX.

B.

Bacon, Lord, fond of gardening 197
Balm of Gilead, cuttings of 70
Beds, forming of 22, 23.—To be turned up for the winter 179
—*See* Borders.
Biennials 55. 102
Bignonia radicans, or Trumpet flower 19
Borders, forming of 18. 25.— Edgings for 27.—To be turned up . . . 179
Botanist, explanation of the term 138.—Its misuse 139
Botany, how far essential to the Gardener . . . 140
Box edgings . . . 42. 155
Brompton stocks 111. 158
Bulbous roots raised from seed 147.—Soil proper for 165.— Natural Economy of 97.— Time for putting them into the ground 164. 180.— Instructions 97. 165, 166.— When to be taken up 96. 127.—Subsequent management of them . . . 96
Bulbous roots in glasses 168
Bulbous roots raised in pots 165
Bulbous roots, autumnal 102

C.

Calceolaria Rugosa 81. 176
Calceolaria, Yellow . 106
Californian Escholtzia . 79
Calycanthus precox . . 19
Campanula Carpatica . 118
Canada Columbine . . 65
Carnations raised from seed 71. 154.—Varieties 123.— Descriptive catalogue of, made from the petals 126. Management of 124. 161. 181.—Cuttings and slips 100.—Layers 120. 125. 144. —Cautions against wet 131. —The Tree variety . 132
Carolina Lily 160
Central bed, designs for 22
Cheiranthus tristis, or Night Stock 82
Chinese Day Lily, *see* Hemerocallis Cærulea.

INDEX.

Chinese Lychnis . . . 82
Christmas Rose . . . 46
Chrysanthemums, propagation of 103
Clarkia Pulchella . . 79
Clematis Florida . . 32
Climates, contrast of . 184
Cloth of gold Crocus . 47
Colchicums, frequently identified with autumnal crocuses 102
Cold Frame 170
Commelina Cœlestis 75. 190
Composts to be prepared 159
Convolvulus major . . 32
Corchorus Japonica . . 33
Creepers 32
Crocuses 47.—Instructions for planting 164
Crocuses, Autumnal 102.—To be distinguished from Colchicums 102
Cuttings, various instructions respecting 80. 86. 99. 101. 126. 146

D.

Dahlias, mode of propagating, 75.—Growth 160. 175.—When to be taken up 188
Dead leaves, useful as manure, 25. 179. 181.
Deciduous plants . . 32
Dianthus superbus 118. 190
Dividing roots of herbaceous plants 148
Draining borders 25.—Plants in pots 61
Dutch style of laying out a Garden 16

E.

Edgings for borders 27. 41. 155
Erinus Lychnidea . . 84
Escholtzia Californica . 79
Ever-blooming Rose . 174
Evergreens 30

F.

Ferraria Tigridia, or Tiger flower 148
Florist, meaning of the term, as distinguished from the epithets "Gardener" and "Botanist" 134
Flowering shrubs, management of . . 39

INDEX.

Florists' Flowers . 42. 137
Fumaria Nobilis . . . 110
Fumaria, Yellow . . 190

G.

Garden, instructions for the formation of a 15. 35.—Work in for January 15; February 35; March 47; April 58; May 75; June 92; July 115; August 132; September 153; October 163; November 178; December 192
Garden and hot-house nosegays contrasted . . 29
Gardener, the, distinguished from the Florist and Botanist 134
Gardening, pleasure afforded by it 29; Promotive of a love of industry, neatness, &c. 116. 196
Geraniums 171
Geum coccineum . . 110
Gravel walks, making of 28. —To be kept clear of weeds 109

Greenhouse plants 80. 88. 125.—Directions for preserving them during the winter 171

H.

Hearts-ease 66
Helleborus Niger, or Christmas rose 46
Hemerocallis Cærulea, or Chinese Day Lily . . . 118
Herbaceous plants 30. 60.— Dividing their roots 148
Hyacinth, the Musk . 89
Hyacinths 49. 67. *See* Bulbous roots.
Hyacinths, management of in glasses 168.—Time for putting them into the ground, 180

I.

Implements for gardening 38
Indian Pinks, laying of 145
Iris Germanica . . . 110
Iris Persica 65

J.

Jasmine 19
Jasminum Revolutum . 32

INDEX.

K.
Kalmia 31

L.
Layers of carnations 120. 125. 144; and of other plants 145
Laying out a Garden 15. 22
Leaves, decayed, their uses as manure . 25. 180. 181
Liatris Scariosa . . 151
Liatris Spicata . . . 151
Liatris Squarrosa . . 151
Light essential to plants 69
Lilac, its mode of flowering 178
Lindley's Œnothera . 79
Lithospermum Orientale 110
Lobelia 151
Lobelia, Blue . . . 88
Lobelia Siphilitica, or Blue American Lobelia . 120
Lobelia splendens . . 108
Lungwort 65
Lychnis Coronaria, or Chinese Lychnis . . . 82

M.
Markers, or sticks, to denote the places of plants, of which the stems die away in autumn . . . 172. 178
Marvel of Peru . . . 188
Miffy, the gardeners' term for flowers that die suddenly 86
Mignonette, preserved through the winter 150
Mimulus rivularis . . 108
Moneywort 108
Multiflora Rose . . . 162
Muscari Moschatum, or Musk hyacinth . . . 89

N.
Narcissus, best situation for 164.—Flowering in glasses 168
Neatness essential in gardening 116. 156
Night Stock 85
Nosegays from the garden and the hot-house, contrasted 29
Nummularia, or Moneywort 108

O.
Ornamental piece for a garden 161

INDEX.

Orobus **Vernus,** or Bitter Vetch 65

P.

Papaver Orientale . . 110
Pasque flower . . . 89
Penstemon 82
Perennials, sowing 55.—Management of the plants 102; their places to be marked in winter 173. 179
Periploca Græca . . . 33
Persian Iris 65
Phlox, various sorts of . 151
Phlox Amœna . . . 118
Phlox Ovata 110
Phlox Pyramidalis . . 160
Phlox Stolonifera . . 118
Petunia, or White Tobacco 81
Pinks, to make pipings of 99. 154
Planting out seedlings . 61
Plants distinguished by their several species 30.—Protected in winter by snow 183
Pleasures afforded by the Garden . 29. 115. 116. 196
Plumbago Capensis . 176

Polyanthus seed, when to be sown 42
Precautions respecting the situations chosen for large shrubs 38
Pruning . . . 40. 173
Pulling up weeds . . 92
Pulmonaria, or Lungwort 65
Pyrus Japonica . . . 32

R.

Ranunculuses, management of 51.—Cautions relative to putting them in the ground 169. 180
Rhododendrons 25. 33. 110.—Caution in pruning them 173
Rock plants 66. 150
Rose, the Christmas 46; the Ever-blooming . . 174
Roses, Standard, how to obtain 128
Rubus Arcticus . . . 111
Russian violet . . . 160
Rustic Flower Basket . 106

S.

Salvia splendens . . 151
Sanguinaria Canadensis 65

Seeds, directions for sowing 42; for gathering and preserving 125. 156
Shrubs, distinguishing characteristics of . . . 30
Slipperwort 81
Slips of herbaceous plants 148
Snow, a preserver of plants 183
Snowdrops 164
Soil proper for different plants 25
Sowing flower seeds 42. 53. 55. 61. 90
Spiderwort, varieties of 118
Spigelia Marylandica . 118
Spring in the Alpine countries 185
Standard Rose-trees . 128
Stocks, when to be sown 111. —Subsequent management 159
Stocks, Night-scented . 176
Succession bed of spring flowers 47
Suckers to be removed and preserved . . . 179
Sweet-williams . . . 145

T.

Tender annuals . 69. 118
Ten-week stocks . . 158
Tiger flower 148
Tobacco, see Petunia.
Tools for Gardening . 38
Tradescantia Virginiana, or Spiderwort 118
Transplanting in autumn 172
Tree carnation . . . 132
Trumpet flower . . . 19
Tulips, instructions respecting 168.—Time for putting into the ground 180. See Bulbous Roots.
Turf, laying of . . . 41
Turf for Shrub Border 25. 159

V.

Vegetable physiology 130. 193
Verbena 71
Verbena Aubletia . . 82
Verbena Melindris . . 82
Vetch, Bitter, see Orobus Vernus.
Violets Autumnal . . 160
Virginian Creeper . . 33

U.

Uvularia 89

INDEX.

W.

Watering plants during autumn and winter . . 175
Wet, cautions against 181. 187
Winterberry tree . . 33

Winter Hellebore, or Yellow Aconite 59

Y.

Yellow Aconite . . . 59
Yellow Gerandia . . 152

THE END.

www.ingramcontent.com/pod-product-compliance
Lightning Source LLC
Chambersburg PA
CBHW021730220426
43662CB00008B/776